A-Z BURTON U

CONTEN

Key to Map Pages	2-3
Map Pages	4-35
Ind... selected Places of Interest	

REFERENCE

A Road	A38
B Road	B5008
Dual Carriageway	
One-way Street Traffic flow on A Roads is indicated by a heavy line on the driver's left.	
Restricted Access	
Pedestrianized Road	
Track	
Footpath	
Residential Walkway	
Railway	Station, Level Crossing, Tunnel
Built-up Area	HIGH STREET
Local Authority Boundary	
Postcode Boundary	
Map Continuation	16

Car Park (selected)	P
Church or Chapel	†
Fire Station	
Hospital	H
House Numbers A & B Roads only	57 44
Information Centre	i
National Grid Reference	320
Police Station	▲
Post Office	★
Toilet with facilities for the disabled	
Educational Establishment	
Hospital or Hospice	
Industrial Building	
Leisure or Recreational Facility	
Place of Interest	
Public Building	
Shopping Centre or Market	
Other Selected Buildings	

Scale
1:19,000

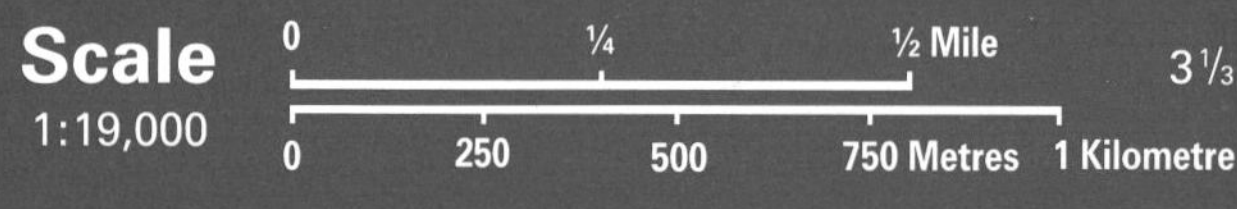

3⅓ inches (8.47 cm) to 1 mile
5.26 cm to 1km

Geographers' A-Z Map Company Ltd.

Head Office:
Fairfield Road, Borough Green, Sevenoaks, Kent TN15 8PP
Telephone: 01732 781000 (General Enquiries & Trade Sales)

Showrooms:
44 Gray's Inn Road, London WC1X 8HX
Telephone: 020 7440 9500 (Retail Sales)

www.a-zmaps.co.uk

Ordnance Survey® This product includes mapping data from Ordnance Survey® with the permission of the controller of Her Majesty's Stationery Office.

Edition 2 2000 Edition 2b (part revision) 2003

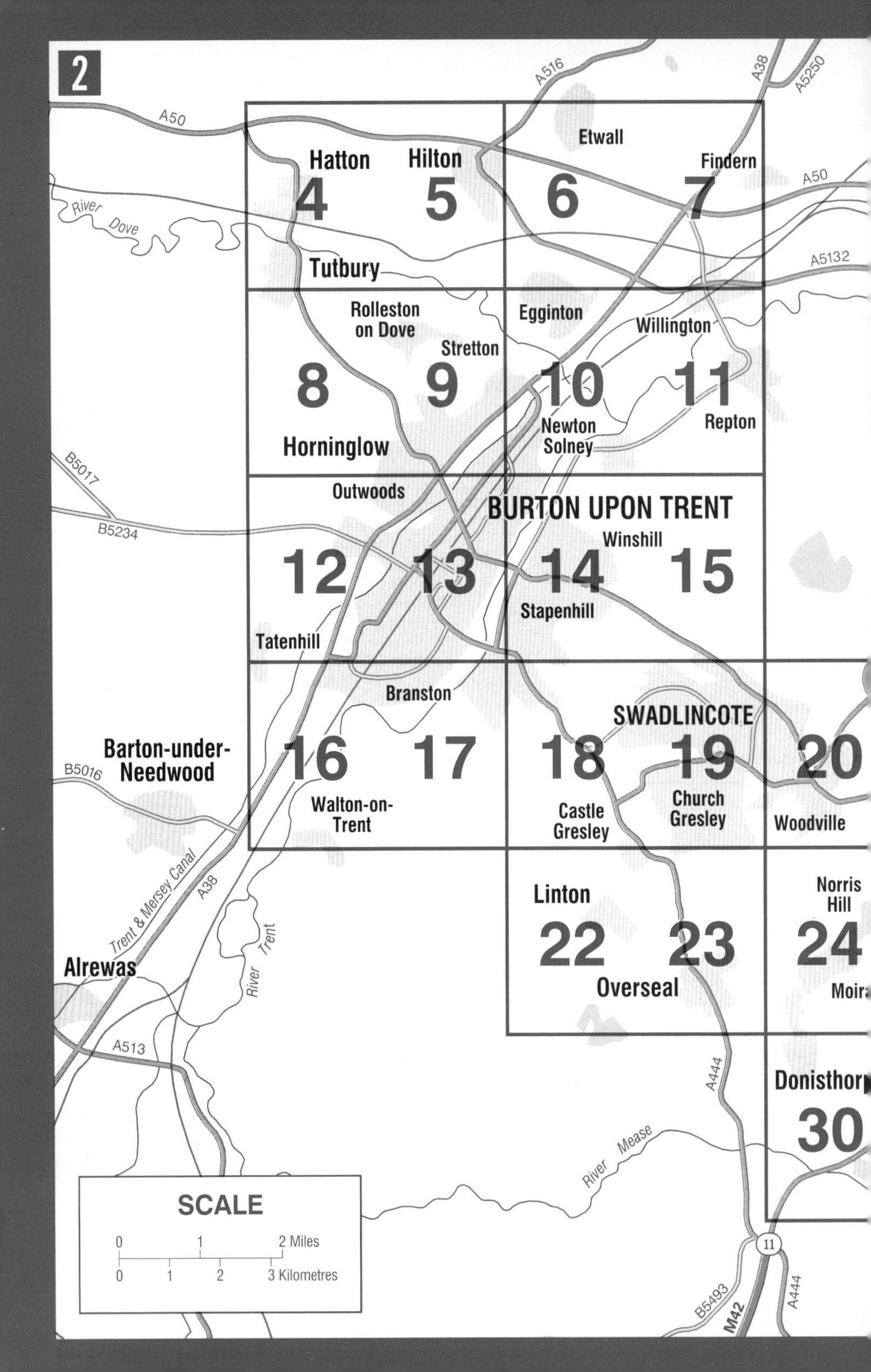
A516
A38
A5250
A50
Etwall
Hatton
Hilton
Findern
4
5
6
7
A50
River Dove
Tutbury
A5132
Rolleston on Dove
Egginton
Willington
Stretton
8
9
10
11
Newton Solney
Repton
Horninglow
B5017
Outwoods
BURTON UPON TRENT
B5234
Winshill
12
13
14
15
Stapenhill
Tatenhill
Branston
SWADLINCOTE
Barton-under-Needwood
B5016
16
17
18
19
20
Walton-on-Trent
Castle Gresley
Church Gresley
Woodville
Trent & Mersey Canal
A38
Linton
Norris Hill
22
23
24
River Trent
Alrewas
Overseal
A513
A444
Donisthorpe
30
River Mease
SCALE
0
1
2 Miles
0
1
2
3 Kilometres
11
B5493
M42
A444

KEY TO MAP PAGES

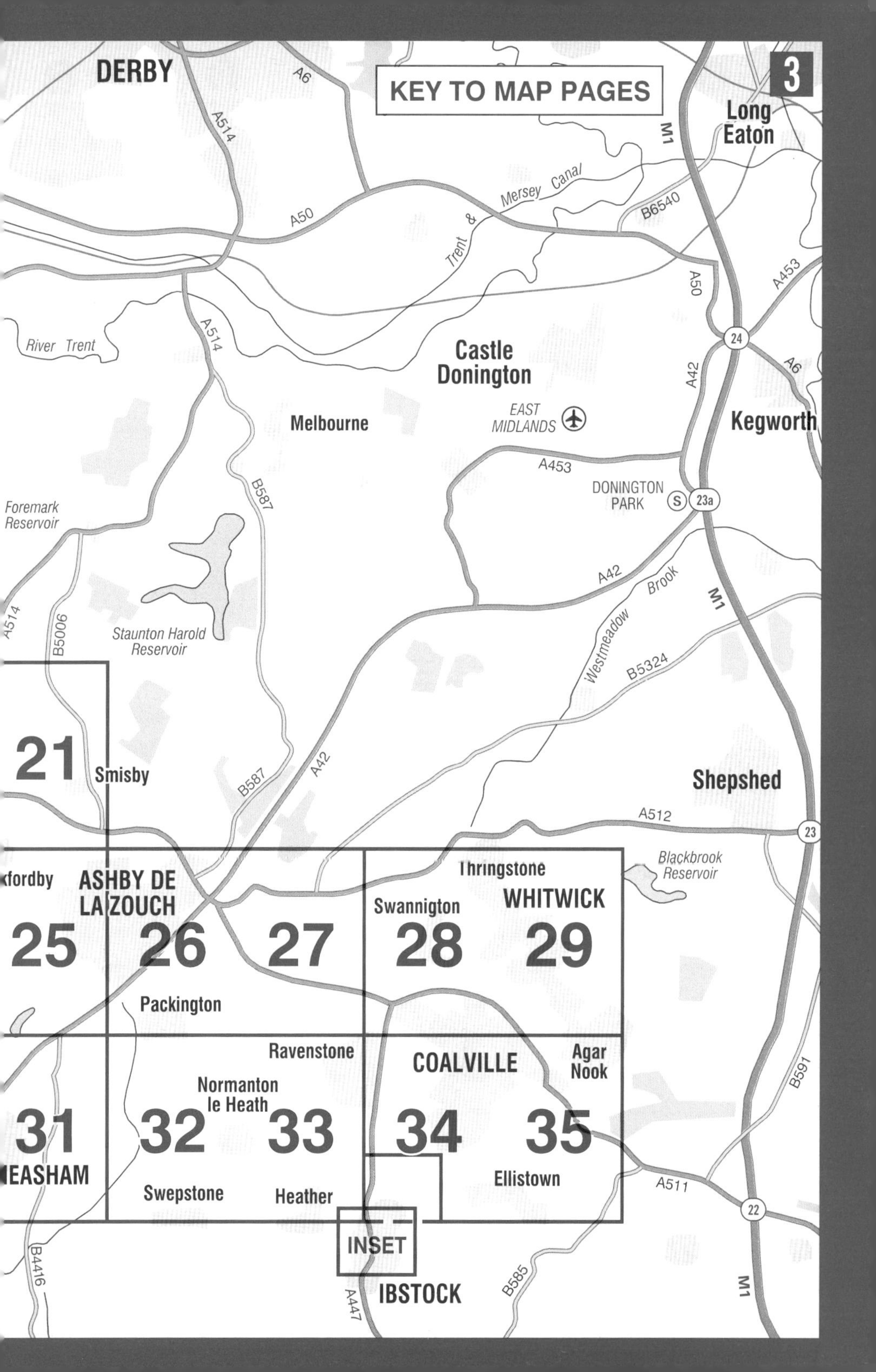

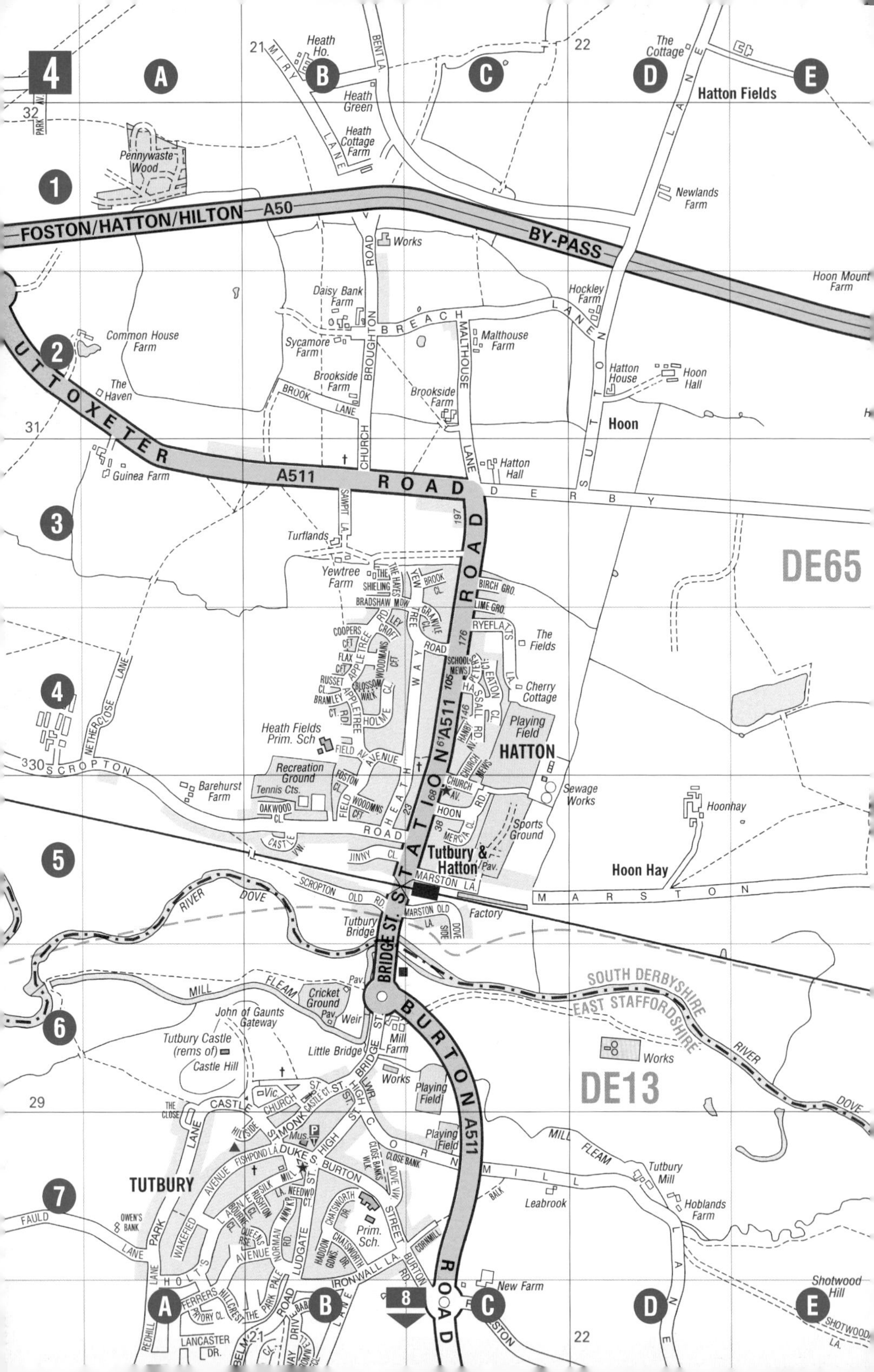

4
A
B
C
D
E
1
2
3
4
5
6
7
8
21
22
32
31
30
29
Heath Ho.
Heath Green
Heath Cottage Farm
MIRY LANE
BENT LA.
The Cottage
Hatton Fields
Pennywaste Wood
PARK AV.
FOSTON/HATTON/HILTON A50 BY-PASS
Newlands Farm
Works
BROUGHTON ROAD
Daisy Bank Farm
BREACH LANE
Hockley Farm
Hoon Mount Farm
Common House Farm
Sycamore Farm
Malthouse Farm
MALTHOUSE LANE
Brookside Farm
BROOK LANE
Hatton House
Hoon Hall
The Haven
UTTOXETER ROAD
CHURCH
Hoon
SUTTON LANE
Hatton Hall
Guinea Farm
A511
DERBY
SAWPIT LA.
Turflands
DE65
Yewtree Farm
THE SHIELING
THE HAYES
YEW TREE
BROOK CL.
BIRCH GRO.
LIME GRO.
BRADSHAW MDW
LEY CROFT
GRANVILLE CL.
RYEFLATTS LA.
The Fields
COOPERS CFT
APPLETREE
WOODMANS CFT
FLAX CFT
RUSSET CL.
BLOSSOM WALK
BRAMLEY CT.
APPLETREE RD.
HOLME CL.
WAY ROAD
SCHOOL MEWS
PETERS CT.
EATON CL.
Cherry Cottage
HASSALL RD.
HAMBY AV.
Playing Field
HATTON
Heath Fields Prim. Sch
FIELD AV.
AVENUE
STATION ROAD
CHURCH MEWS
NETHERCLOSE LANE
SCROPTON
Recreation Ground
Tennis Cts.
FOSTON CL.
Barehurst Farm
CHURCH AV.
Sewage Works
Hoonhay
OAKWOOD CL.
FIELD CL.
WOODMNS CFT
HEATH ROAD
HOON
MERCIA CL.
Sports Ground
CASTLE VW.
JINNY CL.
Tutbury & Hatton
Pav.
Hoon Hay
MARSTON LA.
MARSTON
SCROPTON OLD RD.
RIVER DOVE
MARSTON OLD LA.
DOVE SIDE
Factory
Tutbury Bridge
BRIDGE ST.
SOUTH DERBYSHIRE
EAST STAFFORDSHIRE
MILL FLEAM
Cricket Ground
Pav.
Weir
BURTON
John of Gaunts Gateway
Tutbury Castle (rems of)
Castle Hill
Little Bridge
Mill Farm
Works
RIVER DOVE
DE13
Works
Playing Field
THE CLOSE
CASTLE
Vic.
CHURCH ST.
MONK ST.
CASTLE CT.
HIGH ST.
LWR. HIGH ST.
CORN MILL LANE
HILLSIDE
Mus.
FISHPOND LA.
DUKE ST.
Playing Field
CLOSE BANK
CLOSE BANKS WLK.
DOVE VW.
BURTON STREET
Tutbury Mill
TUTBURY
AVENUE
SILK MILL
RUSHTON CL.
NEEDWD CT.
BALK
Leabrook
Hoblands Farm
FAULD LANE
OWEN'S BANK
WAKEFIELD AVENUE
PARK LANE
QUEENS RSE
NORMAN RD.
LUDGATE
CHATSWORTH DR.
HADDON GDNS.
Prim. Sch.
CORNMILL
BURTON RD.
IRONWALL LA.
HOLT'S LANE
THE PARK PALE ROAD
FERRERS
HILLCREST
PRIORY CL.
BELMONT
LANCASTER DR.
REDHILL
New Farm
ROAD
EGGINTON
Shotwood Hill
SHOTWOOD LA.

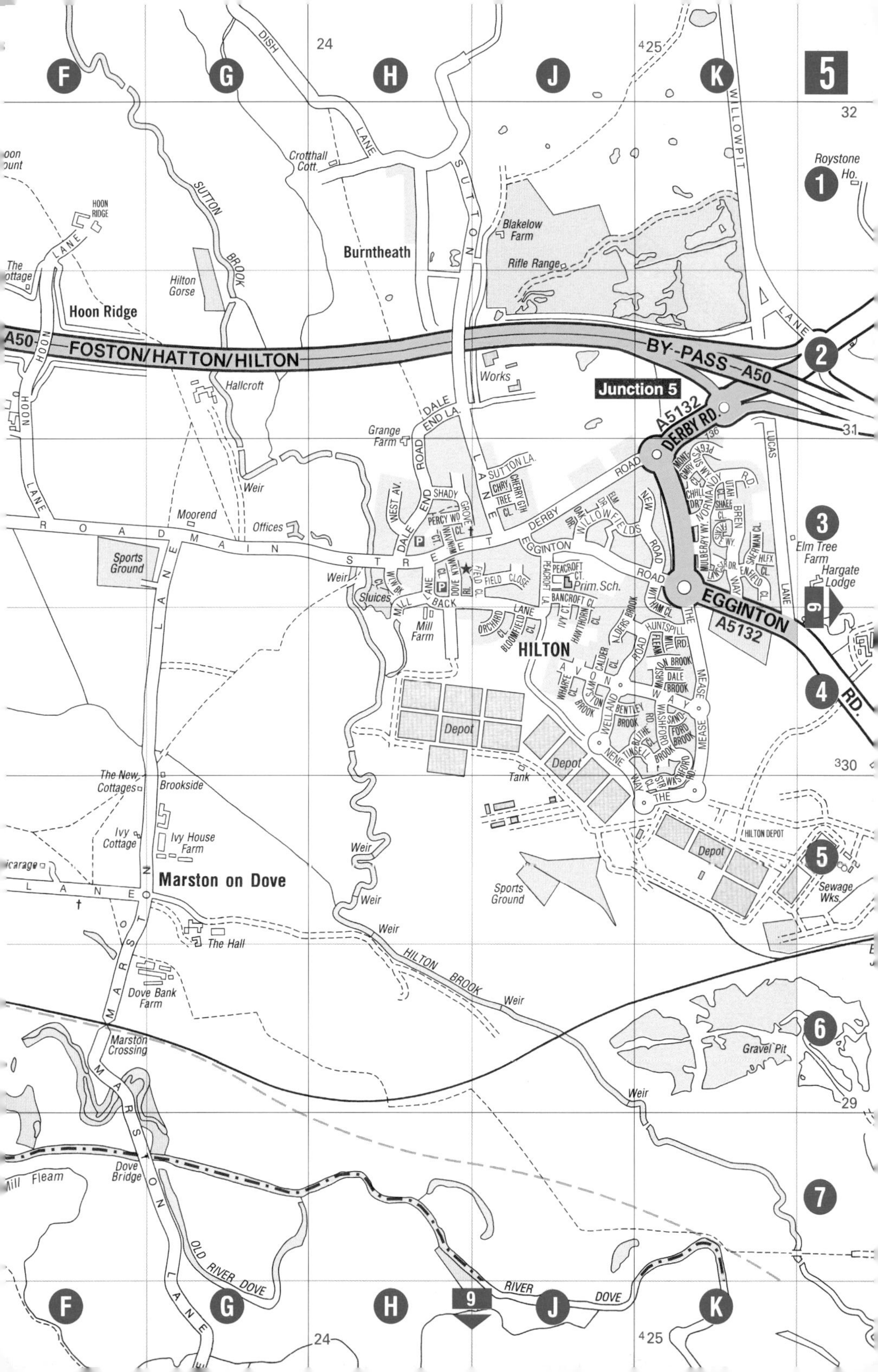

A50 FOSTON/HATTON/HILTON BY-PASS A50
Junction 5
A5132 DERBY RD.
EGGINTON A5132
EGGINTON RD.
Burntheath
Hoon Ridge
HILTON
Marston on Dove
Hilton Gorse
Hallcroft
Blakelow Farm
Rifle Range
Works
Crotthall Cott.
Grange Farm
Moorend
Offices
Sports Ground
Sluices
Mill Farm
Prim.Sch.
Depot
Tank
HILTON DEPOT
Sewage Wks.
Gravel Pit
Elm Tree Farm
Hargate Lodge
Roystone Ho.
The New Cottages
Brookside
Ivy Cottage
Ivy House Farm
The Hall
Dove Bank Farm
Marston Crossing
Dove Bridge
Mill Fleam
OLD RIVER DOVE
RIVER DOVE
HILTON BROOK
SUTTON BROOK
Weir
MAIN STREET
ROAD
HOON LANE
DISH LANE
SUTTON LANE
WILLOWPIT LANE
LUCAS LANE
MARSTON LANE
DALE END ROAD
DALE END LA.
WEST AV.
SHADY GROVE
PERCY WD.
SUTTON LA.
CHERRY TREE CL.
DERBY ROAD
EGGINTON ROAD
NEW ROAD
WILLOWFIELDS
OAK DR.
ELM DR.
BACK LANE
MILL LANE
FIELD CLOSE
PEACROFT CT.
PEACROFT LA.
BANCROFT CL.
IVY CT.
HAWTHORN CL.
ORCHARD CL.
BLOOMFIELD CL.
ALDERS BROOK
CALDER CL.
HUNTSPILL RD.
MILL FLEAM
AVON WAY
WHARFE CL.
WARSTON BROOK
DALE BROOK
WELLAND
BENTLEY BROOK
WASHFORD RD.
SANDFORD BROOK
THE MEASE
NENE WAY
TINSELL BROOK
BLITHE CL.
NORMANDY RD.
MULBERRY WY.
UTAH
BREN WAY
SHERMAN CL.
HLFX CL.
ENFIELD CL.
WITHAM CL.
F G H J K
1 2 3 4 5 6 7
24 425 32 31 330 29
9

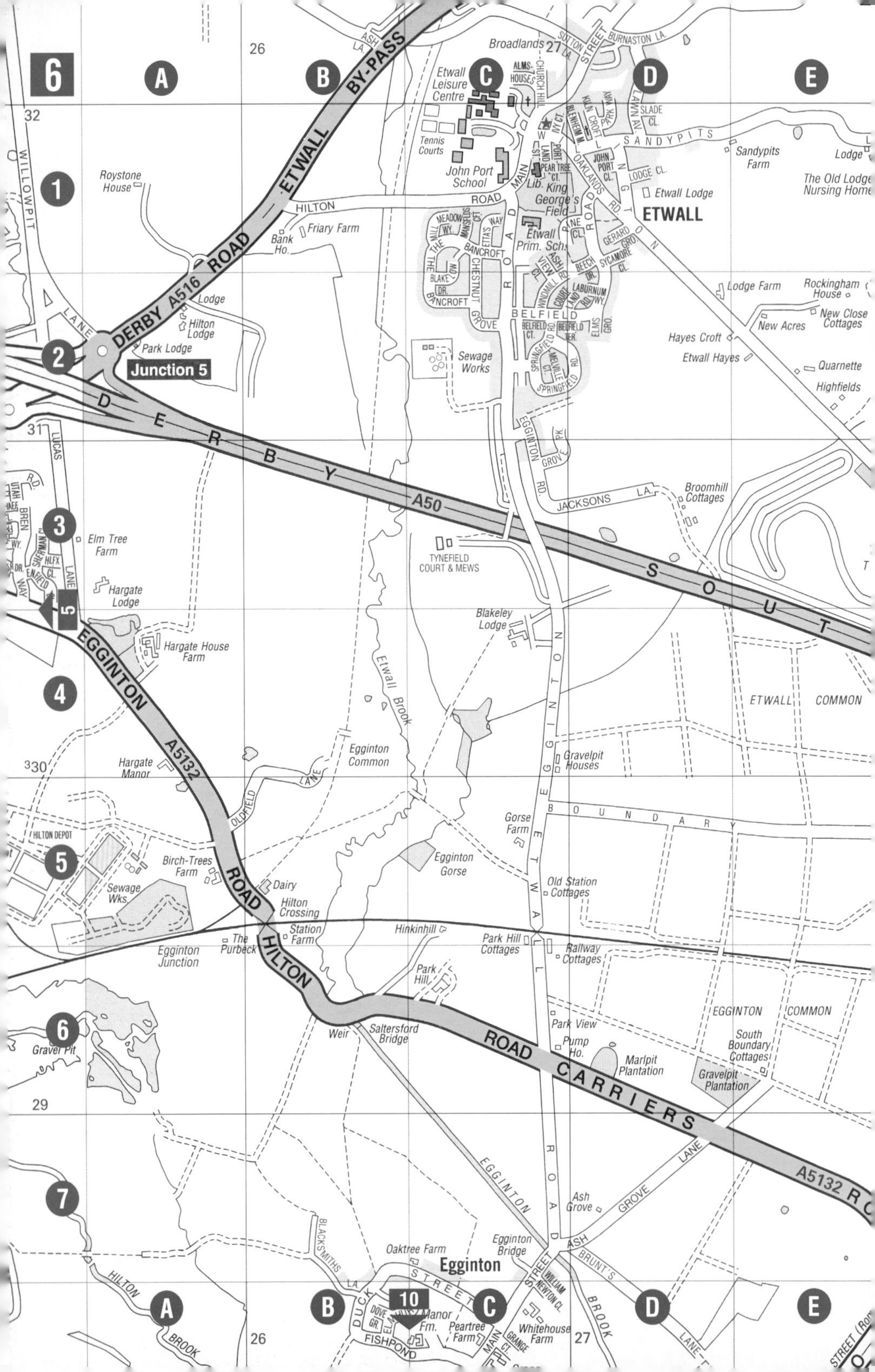

A
B
C
D
E
26
27
32
31
330
29
1
2
3
4
5
6
7
Broadlands
ETWALL BY-PASS
DERBY A516 ROAD
Etwall Leisure Centre
ALMS-HOUSES
CHURCH HILL
SUTTON LA.
STREET
BURNASTON LA.
Tennis Courts
John Port School
Roystone House
HILTON ROAD
Friary Farm
Bank Ho.
Lodge
Hilton Lodge
Park Lodge
Junction 5
WILLOWPIT LANE
Lib.
King George's Field
Etwall Prim. Schs
MAIN ROAD
SANDYPITS
SLADE CL.
LODGE CL.
Sandypits Farm
Lodge
The Old Lodge Nursing Home
Etwall Lodge
ETWALL
OAKLANDS RD.
JOHN PORT CL.
LAWN AV.
PARK WAY
BANCROFT
CHESTNUT GROVE
BELFIELD
SPRINGFIELD RD.
Sewage Works
Lodge Farm
Rockingham House
New Close Cottages
New Acres
Hayes Croft
Etwall Hayes
Quarnette
Highfields
DERBY
A50
SOUT
Broomhill Cottages
JACKSONS LA.
EGGINTON RD.
TYNEFIELD COURT & MEWS
Blakeley Lodge
LUCAS LANE
Elm Tree Farm
Hargate Lodge
Hargate House Farm
5
EGGINTON A5132 ROAD
Etwall Brook
ETWALL COMMON
Egginton Common
Hargate Manor
OLDFIELD LANE
Gravelpit Houses
BOUNDARY
Gorse Farm
HILTON DEPOT
Birch-Trees Farm
Sewage Wks.
Egginton Gorse
Dairy
Hilton Crossing
Old Station Cottages
Station Farm
The Purbeck
Egginton Junction
Hinkinhill
Park Hill Cottages
Railway Cottages
HILTON ROAD
Park Hill
EGGINTON COMMON
Park View
Pump Ho.
Gravel Pit
Weir
Saltersford Bridge
ROAD CARRIERS
Marlpit Plantation
South Boundary Cottages
Gravelpit Plantation
A5132 R
EGGINTON
ETWALL ROAD
GROVE LANE
Ash Grove
Egginton Bridge
BLACKSMITHS LA.
Oaktree Farm
Egginton
DUCK STREET
ASH STREET
WILLIAM NEWTON CL.
BRUNT'S LANE
BROOK
HILTON BROOK
10
Manor Fm.
Peartree Farm
FISHPOND
MAIN
GRANGE CT.
Whitehouse Farm

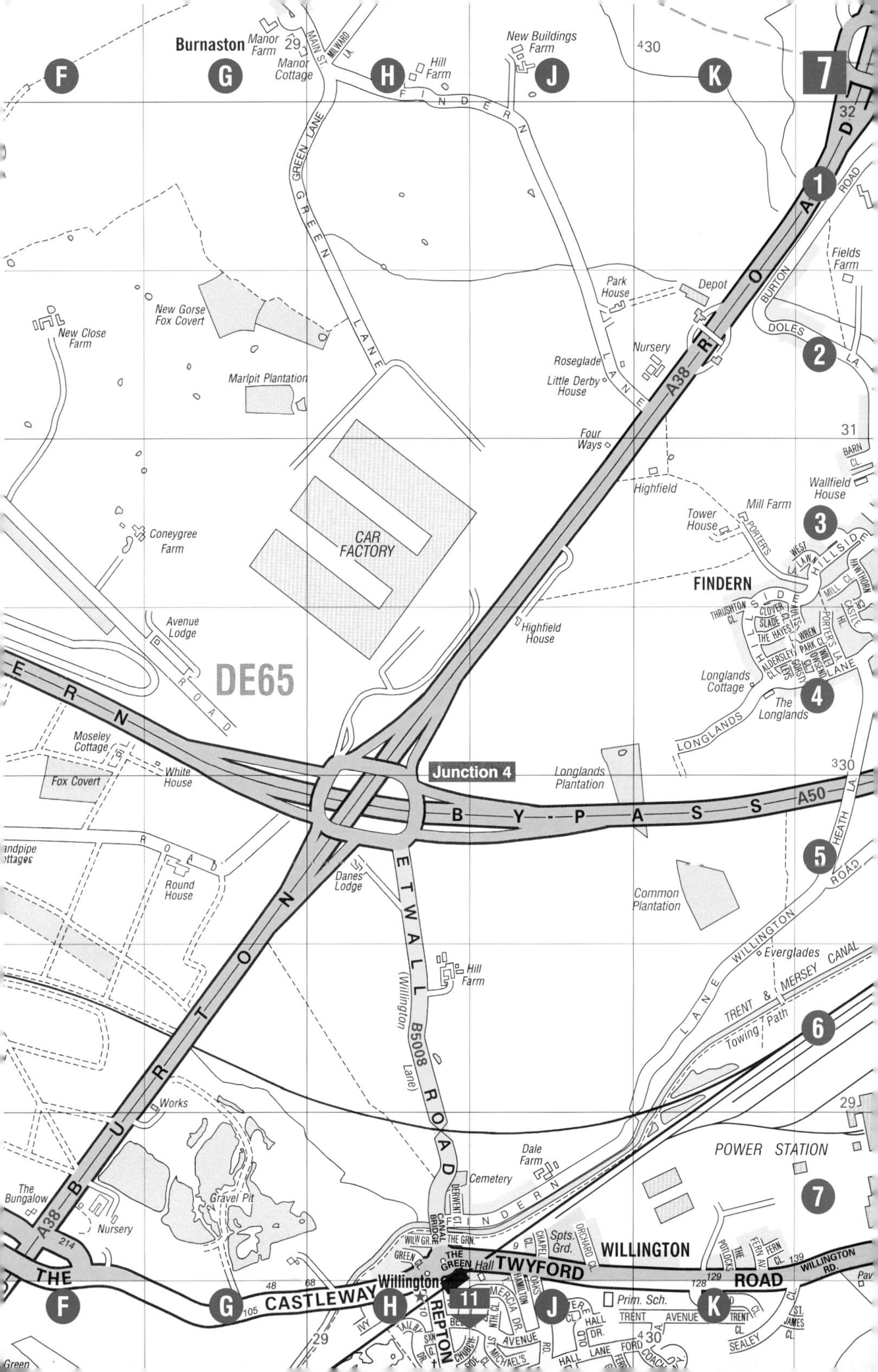
7
Burnaston
Manor Farm
Manor Cottage
Hill Farm
New Buildings Farm
FINDERN
GREEN LANE
New Gorse Fox Covert
New Close Farm
Marlpit Plantation
Park House
Depot
Nursery
Roseglade
Little Derby House
Four Ways
Highfield
Fields Farm
BURTON
DOLES LA.
A38 ROAD
Wallfield House
Mill Farm
Tower House
PORTERS
FINDERN
CAR FACTORY
Coneygree Farm
Avenue Lodge
Highfield House
DE65
Longlands Cottage
The Longlands
LONGLANDS
Moseley Cottage
Fox Covert
White House
Junction 4
Longlands Plantation
BYPASS A50
Round House
Danes Lodge
Common Plantation
HEATH LA.
ETWALL ROAD
(Willington Lane)
B5008
Hill Farm
Everglades
WILLINGTON LANE
TRENT & MERSEY CANAL
Towing Path
POWER STATION
Works
Gravel Pit
The Bungalow
Nursery
Dale Farm
Cemetery
FINDERN
WILLINGTON
TWYFORD ROAD
THE GREEN
Willington
CASTLEWAY
REPTON
Prim. Sch.
TRENT AVENUE
HALL LANE
Spts. Grd.
Junction 4
11

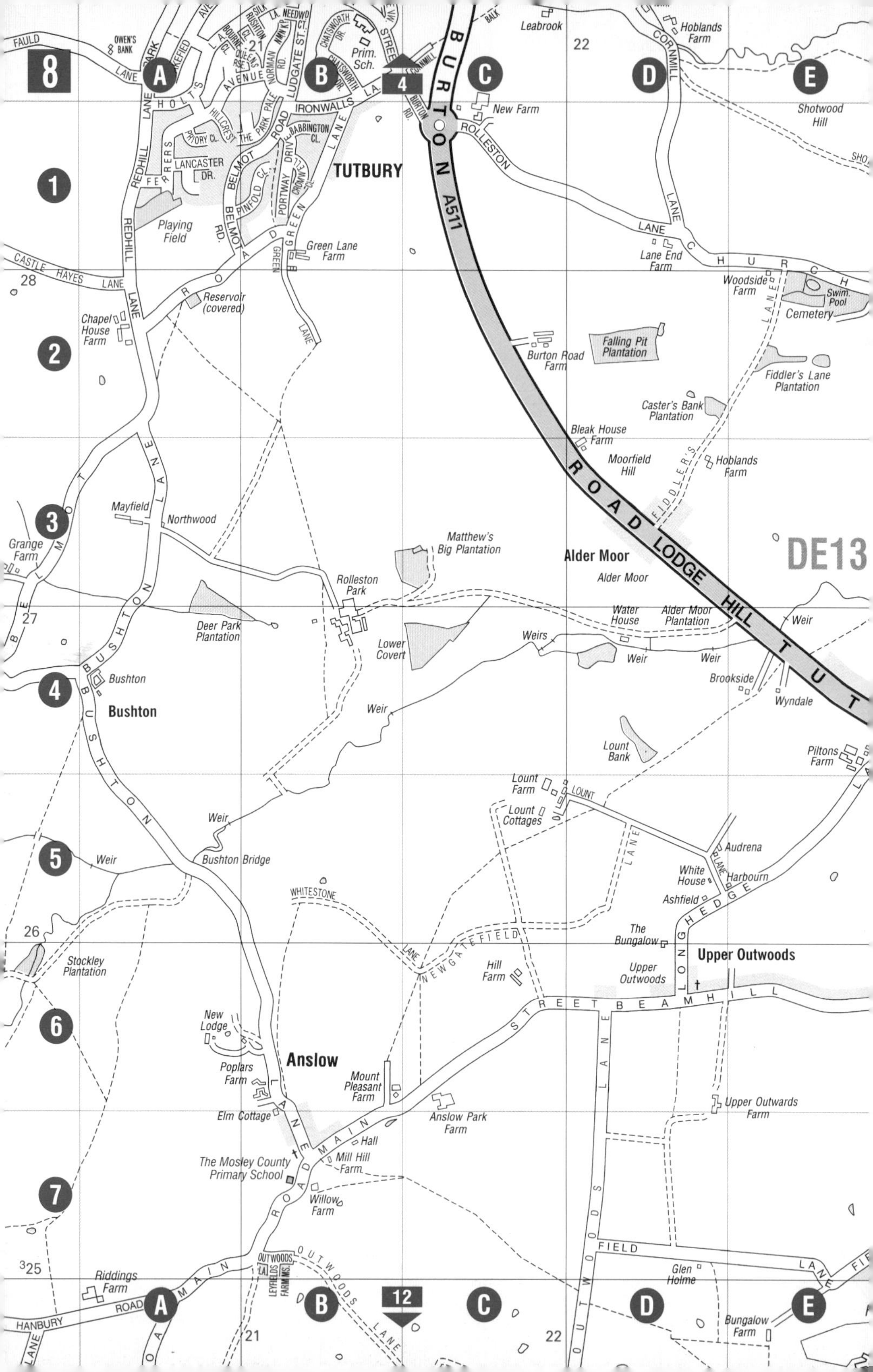

TUTBURY
Bushton
Anslow
Upper Outwoods
Alder Moor
DE13
BURTON ROAD A511
ROAD LODGE HILL TUT
Leabrook
Hoblands Farm
New Farm
Shotwood Hill
Prim. Sch.
Playing Field
Green Lane Farm
Lane End Farm
Woodside Farm
Swim. Pool
Cemetery
Reservoir (covered)
Chapel House Farm
Falling Pit Plantation
Burton Road Farm
Fiddler's Lane Plantation
Caster's Bank Plantation
Bleak House Farm
Moorfield Hill
Hoblands Farm
Mayfield
Northwood
Grange Farm
Matthew's Big Plantation
Rolleston Park
Deer Park Plantation
Lower Covert
Water House
Alder Moor Plantation
Weirs
Weir
Brookside
Wyndale
Lount Bank
Piltons Farm
Lount Farm
Lount Cottages
Audrena
White House
Harbourn
Ashfield
The Bungalow
Bushton Bridge
Stockley Plantation
Hill Farm
Upper Outwoods
New Lodge
Poplars Farm
Elm Cottage
Mount Pleasant Farm
Anslow Park Farm
Upper Outwards Farm
Hall
Mill Hill Farm
The Mosley County Primary School
Willow Farm
Riddings Farm
Glen Holme
Bungalow Farm
FAULD LANE
OWEN'S BANK
PARK
HOLT'S
REDHILL LANE
FERRERS
LANCASTER DR.
PRIORY CL.
HILLCREST
THE PARK PALE
BELMOT ROAD
PINFOLD CL.
PORTWAY DRIVE
GREEN LANE
IRONWALLS LA.
BABBINGTON CL.
CHATSWORTH DR.
LUDGATE ST.
NORMAN RD.
AVENUE
CORNMILL LANE
ROLLESTON LANE
CHURCH LANE
CASTLE HAYES LANE
FIDDLER'S LANE
BELMOT
BUSHTON LANE
WHITESTONE LANE
NEWGATEFIELD LANE
LONGHEDGE LANE
BEAMHILL STREET
MAIN ROAD
OUTWOODS LANE
FIELD LANE
HANBURY ROAD
LEYFIELDS FARM MS.
1 2 3 4 5 6 7
A B C D E
21 22 25 26 27 28
4
12

F
G
H
J
K
24
25
9
5
10
13
1
2
3
4
5
6
7
28
27
26
25
MARSTON LANE
OLD RIVER DOVE
RIVER DOVE
MILL FLEAM
SOUTH DERBYSHIRE
EAST STAFFORDSHIRE
Home Farm
HOME FARM CARAVAN SITE
Sewage Works
Netherfield Grange
Cricket Ground
Rolleston
ROLLESTON ON DOVE
Prim. Sch.
Play. Fld.
John of Rolleston Prim. Sch.
Burton College
Sports Field
Sunnymead Farm
Cliff House
DOVECLIFF ROAD
STATION ROAD
CRAYTHORNE ROAD
BEACON ROAD
BURNSIDE
KNOWLES HILL
BRICK KILN LANE
ANSLOW LANE
Weir
Brook Hollows Spinney
Brook Hollows
Stud Fm.
Beacon Hill
Club House
CRAYTHORNE GOLF CENTRE
Craythorne Farm
Craythorne
Nature Trail
Stretton
Cross Farm
CROSS LANE
Elmleigh
Field Grove Farm
Oaklea
Small Holding
Horninglow Cross
BEAM HILL
The Homestead
BITHAM LANE
BRIDGE LANE
ROLLESTON ROAD
HAREHEDGE LANE
Stretton Play. Fld.
Brook Sch.
Crown Sch.
De Ferrers High Sch. (Lower Site)
De Ferrers High Sch. (Upper Site)
William Hutson Jun. Sch.
Tennis Courts
Playing Field
Rec. Grd.
Castle Park Infant Sch.
Playing Fields
A511
A38
ROAD
GREAVES LANE
BEACONSFIELD ROAD
Horninglow
HORNINGLOW RD. NTH.
Rubber Works
Sports Ground
Eton Park Jun. Sch.
DE14
Club
Rec. Grd.
Burton Albion F.C.
TRENT & MERSEY CANAL
Works
Cricket Grd.
Spts. Grd.
RYKNILD TRADING ESTATE
DERBY ROAD
Outwoods
Sports Ground
Bowling Green
PRINCESS WAY
BEECH LANE

Egginton
Clay Mills
Stretton
Wetmore
DE13
DE14
Ash Grove
Egginton Bridge
Oaktree Farm
Duck Street
Blacksmiths La.
Dove Gr.
Elmhurst
Manor Fm.
Peartree Farm
Fishpond
William
Newton Cl.
Whitehouse Farm
Grange Ct.
Main Lane
Grange Farm
Egginton Prim. Sch.
Smedley Ct.
Church Road
Sewage Works
Benby House
Rotherwood
Brunt's Lane
Egginton Brook
Egginton Brook Bridge
Every Arms Farms
Ryknild Street (Roman Road)
A38
Towing
Hilton Brook
Weir
River Dove
Cliff House
Dove Cliff
Dovecliff Road
Sunnymead Farm
Darfoulde House
Pumping Station
Lodge
High Bridge
Egginton Bridge
Forge Poultry Farm
Forge Lane
Rose Lane
Monk's Bridge
Aqueduct
Derby Road
South Derbyshire
East Staffordshire
Mill Stream
Claymills Rd.
View Av.
Dovecliff Cr.
St. Mary's Dr.
Croydon
Shrewsbury Rd.
Bladon Avenue
Prim. Sch.
Primary Sch.
Hall Green Av.
Jordan Avenue
Gretton Av.
Fairham Rd.
Thorn Dr.
Almond Ct.
Church Rd.
Hall
Cross
Hillfield La.
Moor
Amberlands
Newhay
Furlong
Works
James Brindley Way
Canal
Lane Meadow La.
Filter Beds
Sewage Works
Bowling Green
Recreation Ground
Trent & Mersey
Club
Beech Av.
Eastern Av.
A5121
The Evergreens
Corden Av.
Jackson Av.
Horton Av.
Cricket Grd.
Pav.
Wetmoor Hall Farm
Ryknild Trading Estate
Wetmore Rd.
Riverside
River Trent
B5008
Newton Road
Lodge
Fish Ponds
Newton Park
Bothy Cottage
Cliffe Cottages
Cliffe Lodge
Castle Wood
Bladon Castle
Home Wood
Bladon Hill
Bladon Ho. School
Wranglands Plantation
A B C D E
1 2 3 4 5 6 7
26 27 28 25

6
9
14

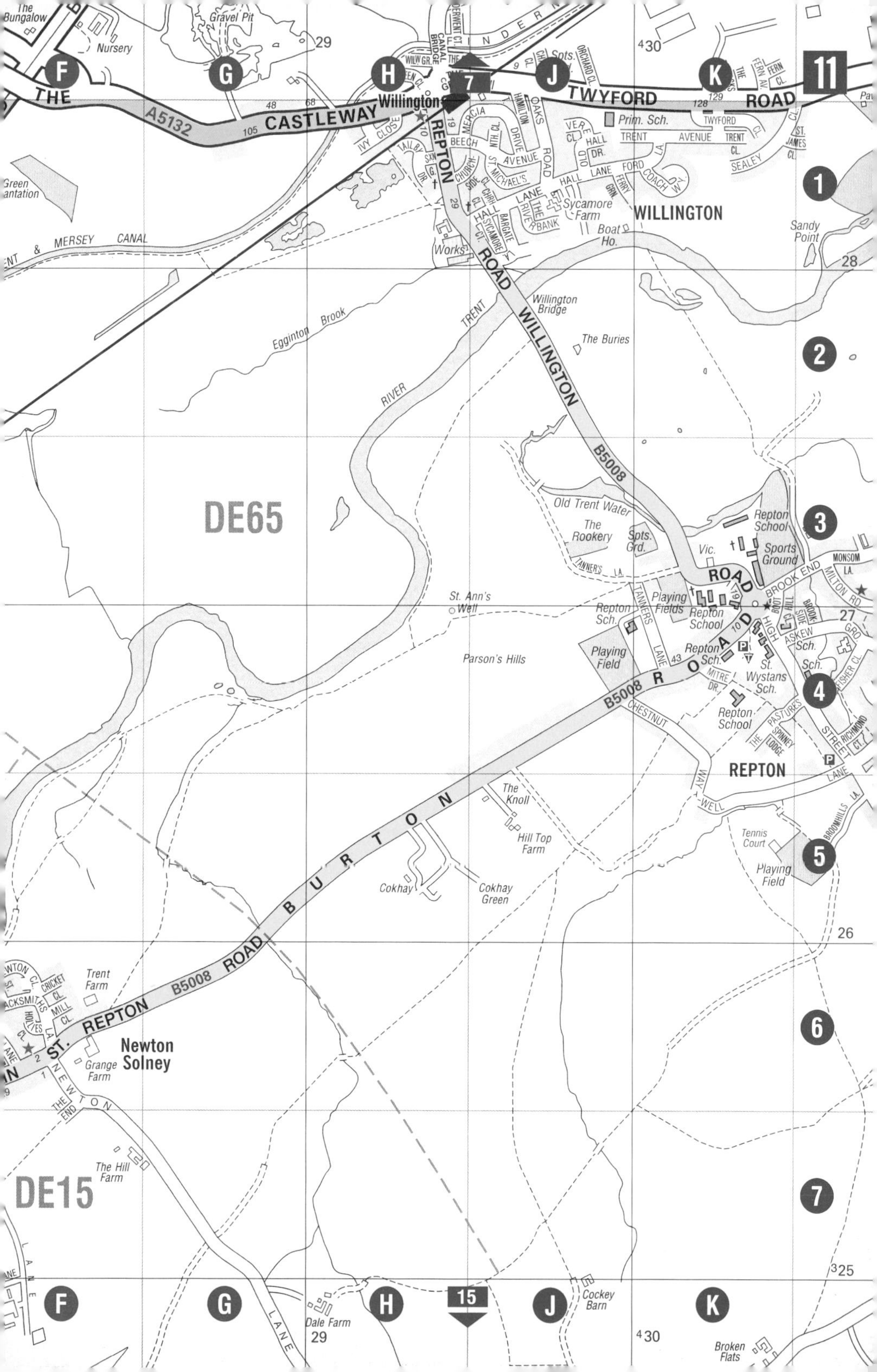
The Bungalow
Gravel Pit
Nursery
THE
A5132
CASTLEWAY
Willington
TWYFORD
ROAD
Prim. Sch.
WILLINGTON
REPTON
ROAD
Green Plantation
TRENT & MERSEY CANAL
Works
Sycamore Farm
Boat Ho.
Sandy Point
Willington Bridge
The Buries
Egginton Brook
RIVER TRENT
WILLINGTON
B5008
DE65
Old Trent Water
The Rookery
Spts. Grd.
Repton School
Sports Ground
Vic.
TANNER'S LA.
Playing Fields
Repton School
Repton Sch.
Playing Field
St. Ann's Well
Parson's Hills
Repton Sch.
St. Wystans Sch.
Repton School
REPTON
B5008
BURTON ROAD
The Knoll
Hill Top Farm
Tennis Court
Playing Field
Cokhay
Cokhay Green
Trent Farm
REPTON ROAD
Newton Solney
Grange Farm
The Hill Farm
DE15
Cockey Barn
Dale Farm
Broken Flats
15
7

12
8
16
DE13
Willow Farm
Riddings Farm
Hanbury Road
Main Road
Outwoods La.
Leyfields Farm Ms.
Outwoods
Field Lane
Glen Holme
Bungalow Farm
Lower Outwoods
Common Farm
Nankirk Lane
Chapel La.
Outwoods Lane
Henhurst Field
Henhurst Wood
Shobnall Brook
Redhouse Farm
Henhurst Hill Pig Farm
Henhurst Wood Farm
Leys Farm
Henshurst Farm
Hopley Road
Reservoirs (covered)
Henhurst Hill Forest Road
B5017
Nursery
Hall
Rough Hay
Playing Field
Henhurst Ridge
Aviation Lane
Council Depot
Postern Road
Shobnall Prim. Sch.
Highcroft Dr.
Reservoir Road
Lordswell Rd.
Sinai Cl.
Bowling Grn.
Anglesey St.
Shobnall Grange
Underpass
Postern House Farm
Glenfield
Sinai Park
Lord's Well
The Rough
A38
Callingwood La.
Pool Green Farm
The Thorns
Prince's Covert
Depot
Common Lane
School Bridge
Street
The Bungalows
Lawns Farm
Works
Warehouse
Seventh Av.
Third Av.
Centrum 100
Second Av.
Wellington
Eighth Av.
Superstore
Centrum East Retail Park
Dark La.
Battlestead Hill
Park Pale
Battlestead Hill Nature Reserve
Hall
Tatenhill
Manor Farm
The Mill House
Branston Lock
Parkway
A5121
Harcourt
Glenley
Spinney Rd.
Warwick Cl.
Harwood Av.
Merlin Cr.
Avenue
Rec. Grd.
Branston
Lawns Farm Cottage
Tatenhill La.
Branston Road
Yews Bridge
The Grove
Brookfields Farm
Towing Path
First Av.
Ninth Av.
Tenth Av.
Offices
Lynwood Rd.
Festival
Clays Rd.
Bridge Av.
Cotswold Rd.
Leamington Rd.
Grave Yard
Branston Bridge

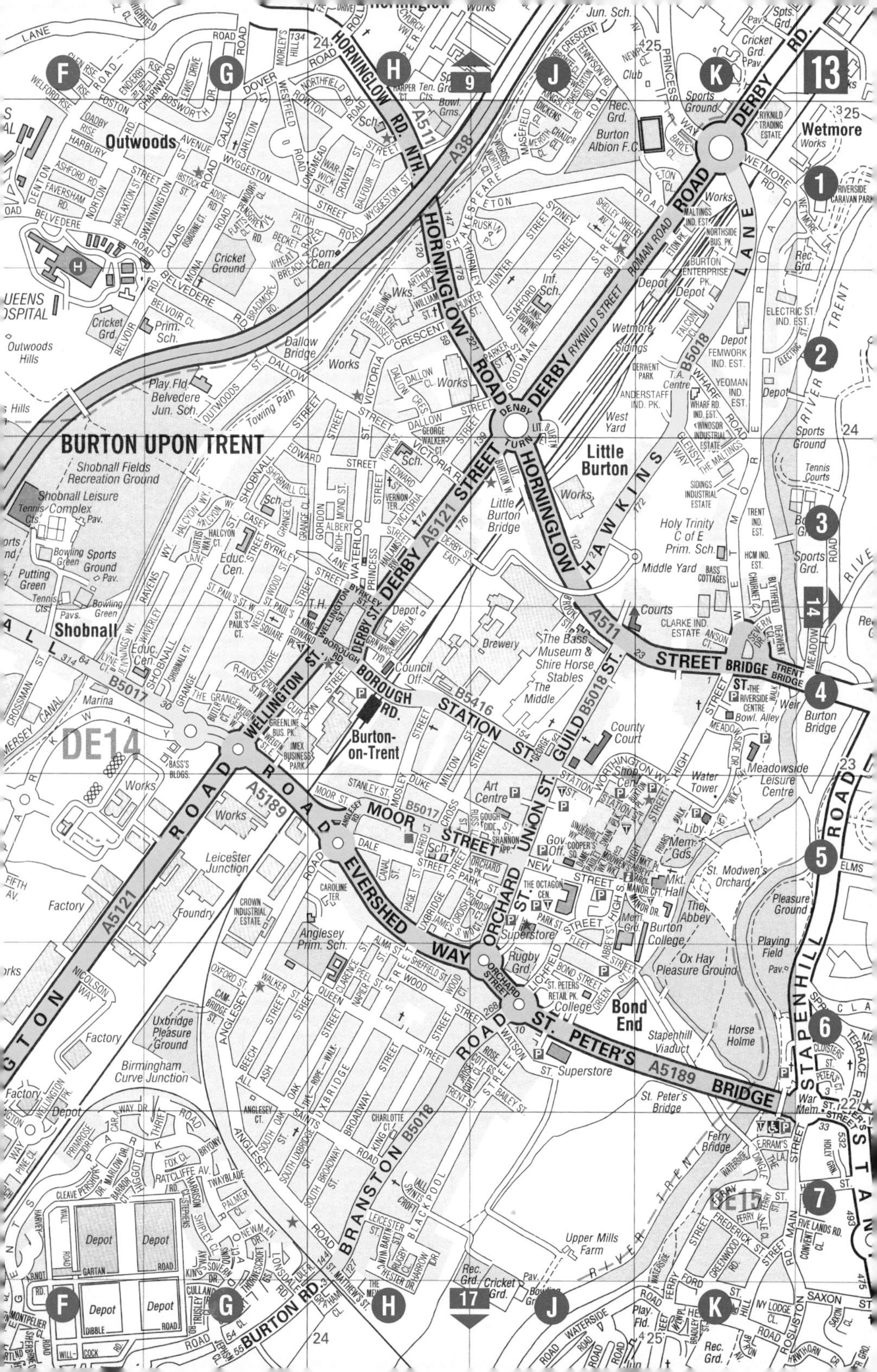

13
9
14
17
F
G
H
J
K
1
2
3
4
5
6
7
BURTON UPON TRENT
Outwoods
Wetmore
Little Burton
Shobnall
Bond End
DE14
DE15
Burton-on-Trent
Shobnall Fields Recreation Ground
Shobnall Leisure Complex
Burton Albion F.C.
The Bass Museum & Shire Horse Stables
Brewery
Council Off.
County Court
Meadowside Leisure Centre
Water Tower
St. Modwen's Orchard
The Abbey
Ox Hay Pleasure Ground
Burton College
Horse Holme
Stapenhill Viaduct
St. Peter's Bridge
Ferry Bridge
Burton Bridge
Trent Bridge
Little Burton Bridge
Dallow Bridge
Upper Mills Farm
Leicester Junction
Birmingham Curve Junction
Uxbridge Pleasure Ground
Anglesey Prim. Sch.
Holy Trinity C of E Prim. Sch.
Middle Yard
West Yard
Wetmore Sidings
Outwoods Hills
Queens Hospital
A38
A511
A5121
A5189
B5017
B5018
B5416
HORNINGLOW RD. NTH.
HORNINGLOW ROAD
DERBY STREET
DERBY ROAD
WELLINGTON ROAD
STATION ST.
BOROUGH RD.
MOOR STREET
EVERSHED WAY
ST. PETER'S BRIDGE
BRANSTON ROAD
HAWKINS LANE
WETMORE ROAD
STAPENHILL ROAD
RIVER TRENT

14
A
B
C
D
E
10
13
18
26
27
1
2
3
4
5
6
7
DE14
Wetmore
WINSHILL
STAPENHILL
Wetmoor Hall Farm
RYKNILD TRADING ESTATE
RIVERSIDE CARAVAN PARK
ELECTRIC ST. IND. EST.
Works
Rec. Grd.
Cricket Ground
Weir
Meadows Farm
Depot
Sports Ground
Tennis Courts
Bowl. Grn.
Sports Grd.
HCM IND. EST.
RIVER TRENT
Recreation Ground
Burton Bridge
TRENT BRI.
A511
A444
B5008
NEWTON ROAD
Abbot Beyne Endowed School (Upper Site)
Abbot Beyne Endowed School (Lower Site)
Playing Fields
Play. Flds.
Pipe Line
Mill Stream
Mill Race
Cliffe Cottages
Castle Woc
Bladon Castle
Bladon Hill
Bladon Ho. School
The Close
The Lodge
The Ridge
Bladon Paddocks
Bladon Farm
Bladon Farm Cottages
Wranglands Plantation
Victory Plantation
Dale Brook
Ford
Ckt. Grd.
Rec. Grd.
MILL HILL LANE
HAWFIELD LANE
ASHBY ROAD
ALEXANDRA ROAD
BEARWOOD HILL ROAD
CHURCH HILL ST.
BLADON ST.
NELSON ST.
Jun. Sch.
Tower View Prim. Sch.
Play. Fld.
Sch.
Woodlands and Washlands Trail
Waterloo Clump
Waterloo Mount
TOWER ROAD
Tower Woods
Cemetery
Scalpcliff Hill
Pleasure Ground
Playing Field
Meadowside Leisure Centre
Horse Holme
STAPENHILL ROAD
STANTON RD.
SPRING TERRACE RD.
CLAY STREET
MALVERN ST.
MALVERN AVENUE
GRAFTON RD.
BEAUFORT RD.
WOODS LA.
Model Dairy Farm
Pit (dis)
Cave
Brizlincote Hall Farm
BRIZLINCOTE LANE
EAST STAFFORDSHIRE
SOUTH DERBYSHIRE
War Mem.
Violet La. Inf. Sch.
The Paulet High School
SAXON ST.
ROSLISTON ROAD
MAIN STREET
HOLLY ST.

F
G
H
11
J
K
29
430
325
Dale Farm
Cockey Barn
Broken Flats
NEWTON
LANE
Beaconhill Plantation
Falders Cottages
Hill Farm
Newton Lane Farm
24
Grafton Smallholding
Newton Mount
KNIGHTS LANE
DE15
Bretby Nurseries
Town Farm
Shades Farm
THE SQUARE
Vicarage
Common Farm
Pease-hill
Bretby Mount
Bretby
MOUNT ROAD
THE GREEN
Wood View
Bretby Castle (site of)
War Memorial
WATERY LANE
OLDICOTE LANE
Gas Compound
Home Farm
Philosopher's Wood
23
Oldicote Farm
BRETBY MEWS
Crematorium
The Decoy
Nursing Home
Fish Ponds
BURTON-ON-TRENT GOLF COURSE
Geary House
Club House
The Gorse
The Levelling
WAGGON
BRETBY PARK
Fish Pond
GEARY
Stockings Plantation
STANHOPE GRN
Stanhope Bretby
Bretby Court
ROAD
A511
EAST
BURTON
ROAD
22
THORN TREE LANE
Four Winds
Buckwheat Plantation
Play. Fld.
LANE
DE11
Park Gate Farm
Pottery Works
Broadfield
BRETBY BUSINESS PARK
STANHOPE GLADE
Upper Midway
19
ASTON
THE HIVES
HILTON CL.
HAY
Lee Wood
Windmill Spinney
SUNNYSIDE
WOOD
ROSE TREE
HOLLY BANK CL.
NEWTON PK.
1
2
3
4
5
6
7

Lawns Farm Cottage
Yews Bridge
BRANSTON ROAD
12
Brookfields Farm
Towing Path
PARK-WAY
FIRST AV.
NINTH AV.
TENTH AV.
HARWOOD
MERLIN CR.
AVENUE
LANE
Rec. Grd.
COTSWOLD RD.
BRANSTON
Offices
A38
A5121
FESTIVAL RD.
LYNWOOD RD.
BRIDGFORD AV.
Branston Bridge
ROAD
TATENHILL LA.
Subway
Sch.
LEAMINGTON RD.
Grave Yard
MAIN STREET
B5018
Manor Farm
COURT FARM LA.
OLD ROAD
CHURCH RD.
BRAMELL CL.
WARREN
LANSDOWNE RD.
RIVERSIDE DR.
Visitor Centre
HOLLYHOCK WAY
WOODBINE CL.
CLOVER CT.
TRENT & MERSEY CANAL
BRANSTON WATER PARK
EAST STAFFORDSHIRE
SOUTH DERBYSHIRE
NATURE RESERVE
Tatenhill Lock
Pipe Bri.
Works
Gravel Pit
Gallow Bridge
DE13
Black Meadow Wood
Gorse Hall
Gorsehall Plantation
Newbold Farm
Warren Clump
RYKNILD STREET
ROMAN ROAD
RIVER TRENT
Drakelow Park
Tucklesholme Farm
Newbold Manor Farm
Warren Barn
LICHFIELD ROAD
Sewage Works
Warren Hill
Depot
Motel
Barton Turn
Warren Farm
Rylance Farm
STATION ROAD
Barr Hall
Cricket Ground
Pav.
Walton Bridge
Rectory
STATION LA.
WALTON-ON-TRENT
DE12
RIVERSIDE
MAIN
MEWIES CL.
BELLS END
LADLE END LA.
ORCHARD CL.
HARBIN RD.
Hill Croft
Barn Farm
COTON ROAD
ROSLISTON ROAD
STANDING BUTTS CL.
Walton-on-Trent C. of E. Prim. Sch.
Fairfield
A B C D E
1 2 3 4 5 6 7
21 22 20 19 18

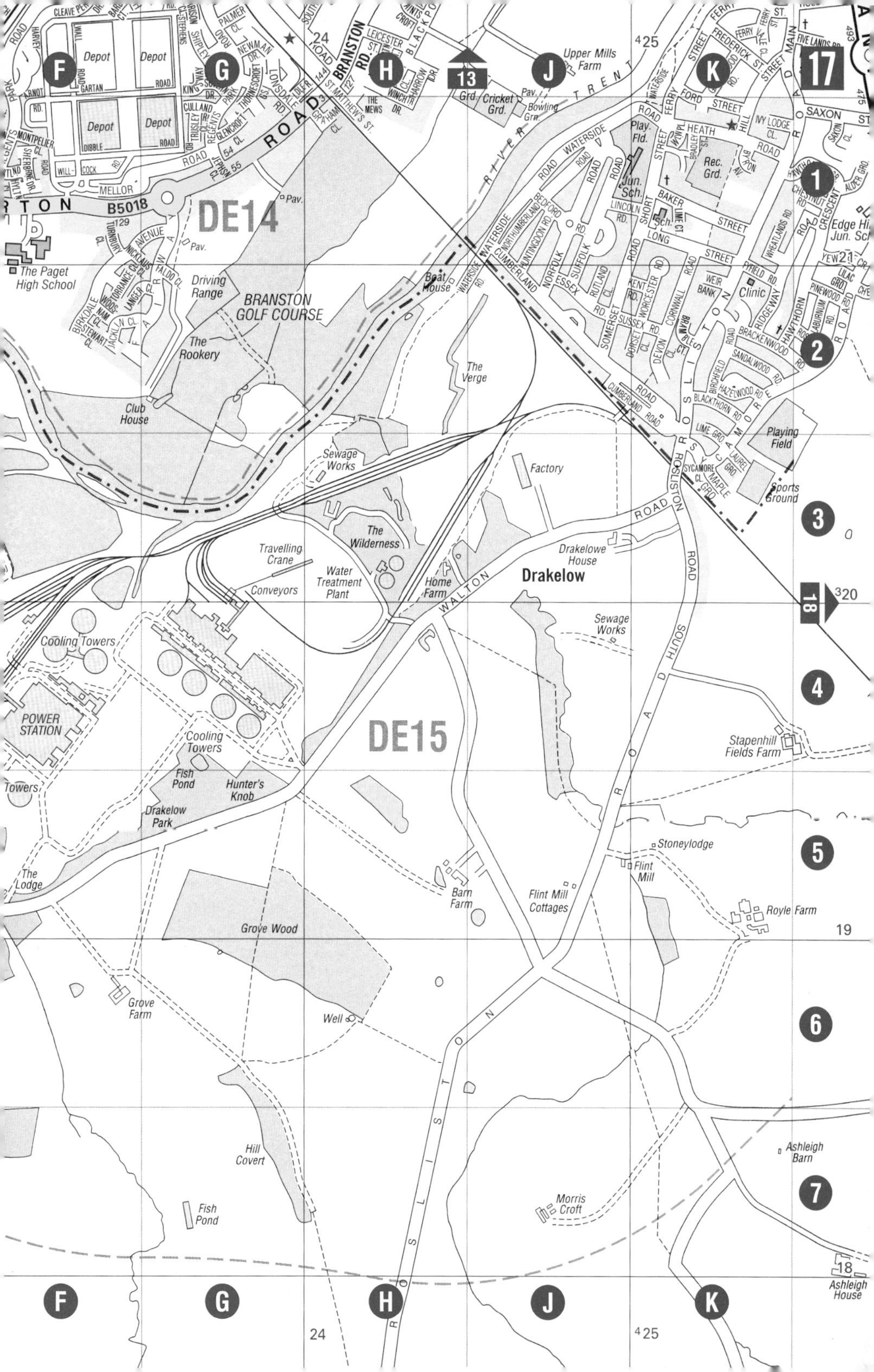
DE14
DE15
BRANSTON GOLF COURSE
Driving Range
The Rookery
Club House
Drakelow
Drakelowe House
Sewage Works
The Wilderness
Travelling Crane
Conveyors
Water Treatment Plant
Home Farm
Factory
The Verge
Boat House
Cooling Towers
POWER STATION
Fish Pond
Hunter's Knob
Drakelow Park
The Lodge
Grove Wood
Grove Farm
Well
Hill Covert
Barn Farm
Flint Mill Cottages
Flint Mill
Stoneylodge
Royle Farm
Stapenhill Fields Farm
Morris Croft
Ashleigh Barn
Ashleigh House
Upper Mills Farm
Cricket Grd.
Bowling Grn.
RIVER TRENT
The Paget High School
Depot
B5018
WALTON ROAD
ROSLISTON ROAD
ROSLISTON ROAD SOUTH
Playing Field
Sports Ground
Clinic
Rec. Grd.
Jun. Sch.
Play. Fld.
Edge Hill Jun. Sch.
Pav.
13
18
F G H J K
1 2 3 4 5 6 7
24
425
320
19

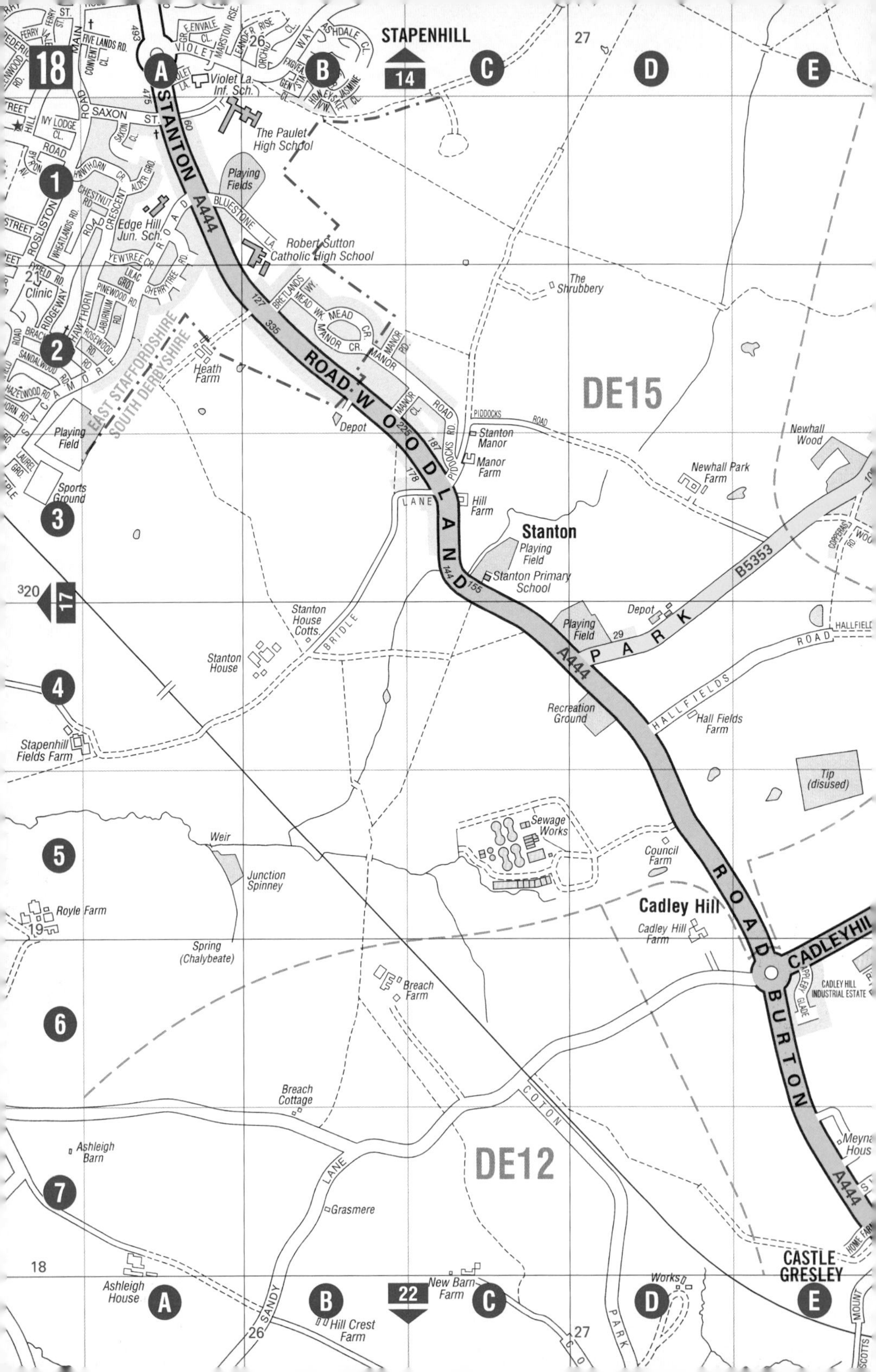
STAPENHILL
14
STANTON
A444
ROAD
WOODLAND
BURTON ROAD
PARK
B5353
HALLFIELDS
HALLFIELD
CADLEYHILL
Violet La. Inf. Sch.
The Paulet High School
Playing Fields
Robert Sutton Catholic High School
Edge Hill Jun. Sch.
Clinic
EAST STAFFORDSHIRE
SOUTH DERBYSHIRE
Heath Farm
Depot
Playing Field
Sports Ground
The Shrubbery
DE15
Stanton Manor
Manor Farm
Hill Farm
Newhall Wood
Newhall Park Farm
Stanton
Playing Field
Stanton Primary School
Stanton House Cotts.
Stanton House
BRIDLE
Depot
Recreation Ground
Hall Fields Farm
Stapenhill Fields Farm
Tip (disused)
Weir
Junction Spinney
Sewage Works
Council Farm
Cadley Hill
Cadley Hill Farm
Royle Farm
Spring (Chalybeate)
Breach Farm
CADLEY HILL INDUSTRIAL ESTATE
APPLEBY GLADE
Breach Cottage
COTON
Ashleigh Barn
DE12
SANDY LANE
Grasmere
Ashleigh House
New Barn Farm
Hill Crest Farm
Works
PARK
CASTLE GRESLEY
HOME FARM
MOUNT
SCOTTS
22
17
320
VIOLET
SAXON ST.
MAIN
ROSLISTON
RIDGEWAY
HAWTHORN
SYCAMORE
BLUESTONE LA.
BRETLANDS WY.
MEAD WK.
MEAD CR.
MANOR CR.
MANOR RD.
MANOR CL.
PIDDOCKS RD.
PIDDOCKS ROAD
LANE
A B C D E
1 2 3 4 5 6 7
26 27 18 19 21 29

19
15
20
23
DE11
NEWHALL
SWADLINCOTE
CHURCH GRESLEY
Albert Village
Upper Midway
BURTON ROAD
A511
EAST
WILLIAM NADINS WAY
A514
CIVIC WAY
HIGH STREET
MAIN ROAD
UNION RD.
B5353 ROAD
MIDWAY
CHURCH ST.
B586
DERBY RD.
HEARTHCOTE RD.
GRESLEY WOOD RD.
GEORGE ST.
YORK RD.
OAK ST.
HALL ST.
REGENT ST.
MARKET ST.
COMMON ROAD
COPPICE SIDE
MAIN ST.
CASTLE ROAD
STATION STREET
PRINCESS ST.
BRETBY BUSINESS PARK
Park Gate Farm
Broadfield
Pottery Works
Windmill Spinney
William Allitt School
Newhall Jun. School
Newhall Inf. Sch.
Lee Wood
Midway Farm
Elmsleigh Infant School
Football Ground
Fairmeadows Prim. Sch.
Training Centre
Hostel
Cemetery
Playing Field
The Pingle School
Eureka Park
Workshop
Depot
Breach Leys Farm
Superstore
HEARTHCOTE ROAD IND. EST.
Council Offices
Leisure Cen.
GEORGE HOLMES BUSINESS PARK
Works & Research Laboratories
BOARDMAN'S IND. EST.
The Woodlands
Kids Rough
Gresley Wood
Pennine Way Junior School
Ski Centre
Jack i' th' Holes
Gresley Common
Memorial Park
Bandstand
Sports Ground
Gresley Old Hall (Miners Welfare)
Hall Wood
Gresley Rovers F.C.
Church Gresley St.George C.of E. Prim.Sch.
Cappy Farm
Sewage Pumping Station
CHURCH GRESLEY IND. EST.
Recreation Ground
Play. Fld.
430
320

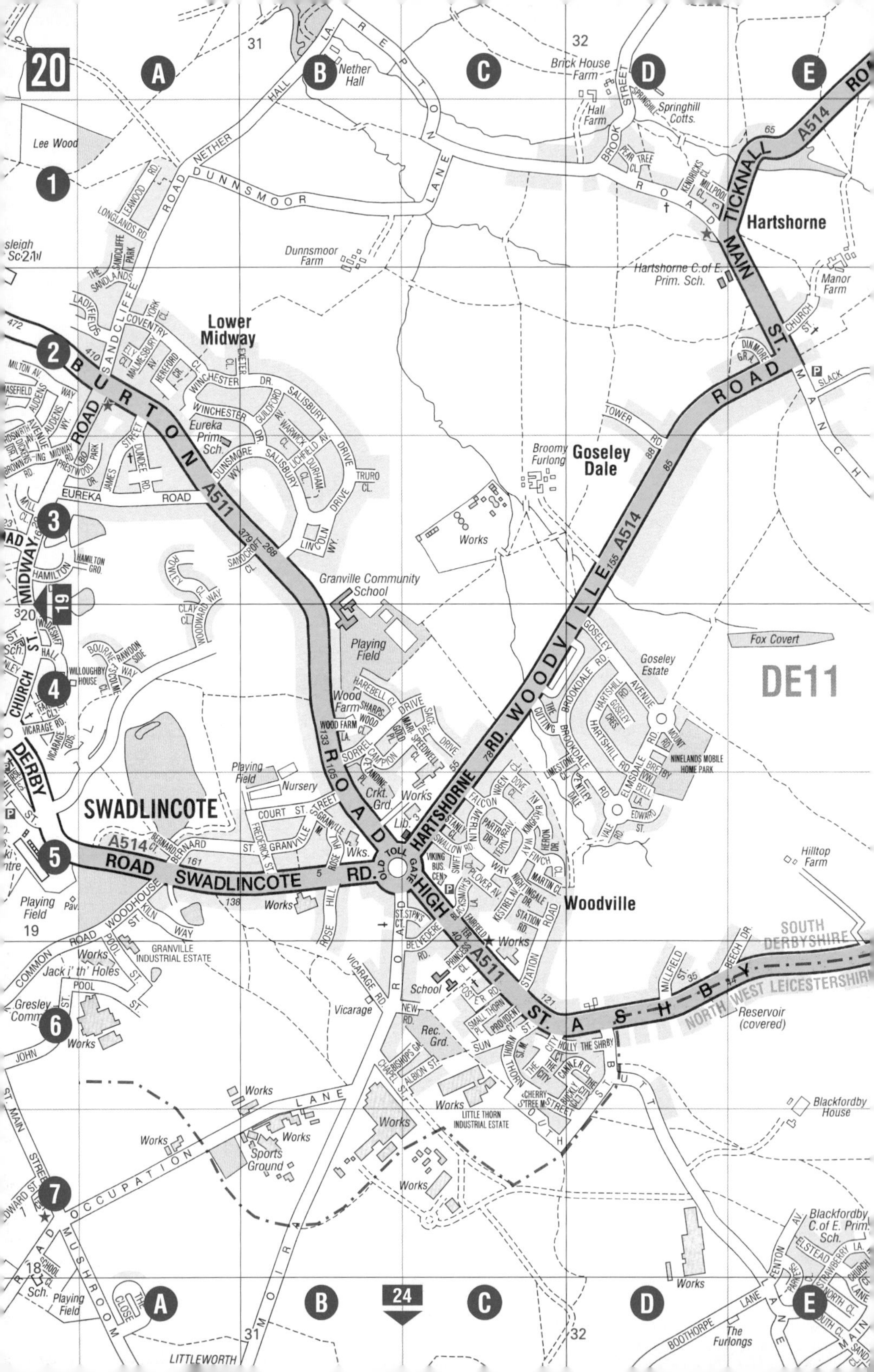

A
B
C
D
E
1
2
3
4
5
6
7
31
32
Nether Hall
Brick House Farm
Hall Farm
Springhill Cotts.
Lee Wood
Dunnsmoor Farm
Hartshorne
Hartshorne C.of E. Prim. Sch.
Manor Farm
Lower Midway
Eureka Prim. Sch.
Broomy Furlong
Goseley Dale
Works
Granville Community School
Playing Field
Fox Covert
Goseley Estate
DE11
Wood Farm
NINELANDS MOBILE HOME PARK
Nursery
Crkt. Grd.
SWADLINCOTE
Woodville
Hilltop Farm
SOUTH DERBYSHIRE
NORTH WEST LEICESTERSHIRE
Reservoir (covered)
GRANVILLE INDUSTRIAL ESTATE
Jack i' th' Holes
Vicarage
Rec. Grd.
School
LITTLE THORN INDUSTRIAL ESTATE
Sports Ground
Blackfordby House
Blackfordby C.of E. Prim. Sch.
The Furlongs
LITTLEWORTH
BURTON ROAD
A511
A514
SWADLINCOTE ROAD
HARTSHORNE ROAD
WOODVILLE RD.
TICKNALL ROAD
MAIN ST.
ASHBY RD.
HIGH ST.
OCCUPATION LANE
MOIRA ROAD
MUSHROOM LANE
REPTON LANE
DUNNSMOOR ROAD
NETHER HALL LA.
BROOK STREET
EUREKA ROAD
MIDWAY
CHURCH ST.
DERBY ST.
24
19

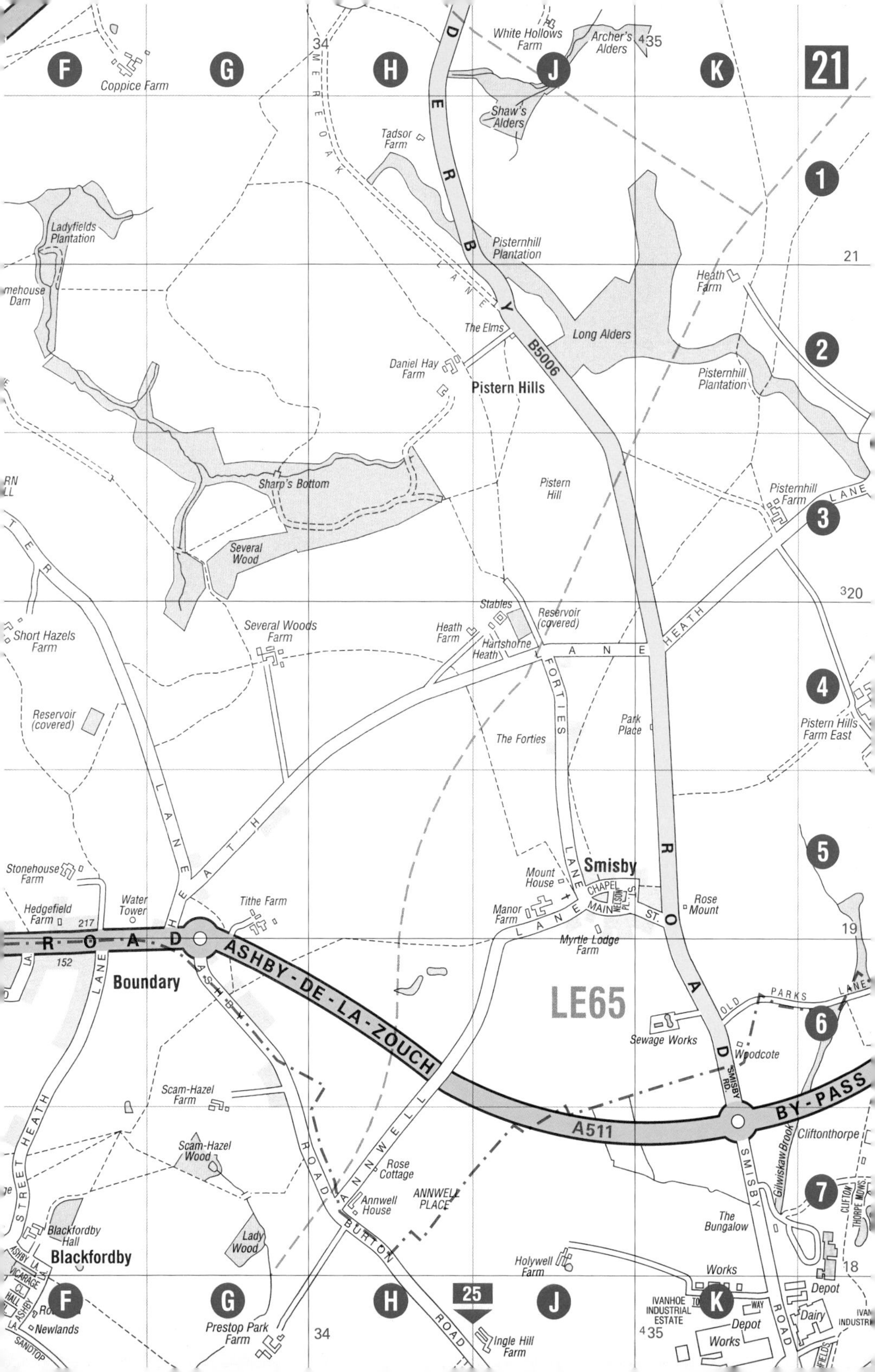
F
G
H
J
K
Coppice Farm
White Hollows Farm
Archer's Alders
Shaw's Alders
Tadsor Farm
MEREOAK LANE
DERBY ROAD
B5006
Ladyfields Plantation
Pisternhill Plantation
Heath Farm
Long Alders
The Elms
Daniel Hay Farm
Pistern Hills
Pisternhill Plantation
Sharp's Bottom
Pistern Hill
Pisternhill Farm
Several Wood
Stables
Reservoir (covered)
Several Woods Farm
Heath Farm
Hartshorne Heath
LANE
HEATH
Short Hazels Farm
Reservoir (covered)
FORTIES
The Forties
Park Place
Pistern Hills Farm East
Smisby
Stonehouse Farm
Mount House
CHAPEL
NELSON PL.
MAIN ST.
Rose Mount
Water Tower
Tithe Farm
Hedgefield Farm
Manor Farm
Myrtle Lodge Farm
ROAD
ASHBY-DE-LA-ZOUCH
Boundary
LE65
OLD PARKS LANE
Sewage Works
Woodcote
SMISBY RD.
Scam-Hazel Farm
A511
BY-PASS
Cliftonthorpe
Scam-Hazel Wood
ANNWELL
Rose Cottage
Gilwiskaw Brook
STREET HEATH
Annwell House
ANNWELL PLACE
The Bungalow
CLIFTON THORPE MDWS.
Blackfordby Hall
Lady Wood
BURTON
Blackfordby
Holywell Farm
Works
Depot
IVANHOE INDUSTRIAL ESTATE
Depot
Dairy
Works
Newlands
SANDTOP
Prestop Park Farm
Ingle Hill Farm
ROAD
SMISBY ROAD
Boundary
1
2
3
4
5
6
7
21
320
19
18
34
435
217
152

25

18
Ashleigh House
Grasmere
SANDY LANE
Hill Crest Farm
New Barn Farm
Works
CASTLE GRESLEY
COTON PARK
Coton Park
Sewage Works
Works
Priory Farm
Manor Farm
Caldwell
CHURCH LA.
MAIN ST.
Caldwell Hall School
Caldwell Covert
Recreation Ground
PARKSIDE
Grange Farm
Manor Farm
Manor House
PARK CL.
CALDWELL ROAD
MAIN STREET
HILLSIDE
CRESTA
WARREN DR.
HIGHFIELDS DR.
PEAR TREE DR.
GREENFIELD DR.
CHESTFLD DR.
SEAL VW.
CEDAR GRO.
AV.
THE CLOSE
PRINCESS
Rec. Grd.
Vic.
WINCHESTER DR.
CHARLTON CL.
SYCAMORE
WINDSOR RD.
PATRICK CL.
EMERY CL.
HELSTON CL.
WEATHER
Privet Plantation
Longlands
Blakenhall Farm
LINTON
Sports Field
DE12
HIGH
Sludge Lagoons
Far Close Farm
Netherleigh
COLLIERY LANE
Oak Dene
Woodside Farm
Hill
Botany Bay Farm
Botany Bay
Park Farm
FLATS LANE
CRAFTY
COALPIT LA.
Potter's Wood
The Ashes
GRANGE WOOD
Church Flatts Farm
26
27
16
17
315

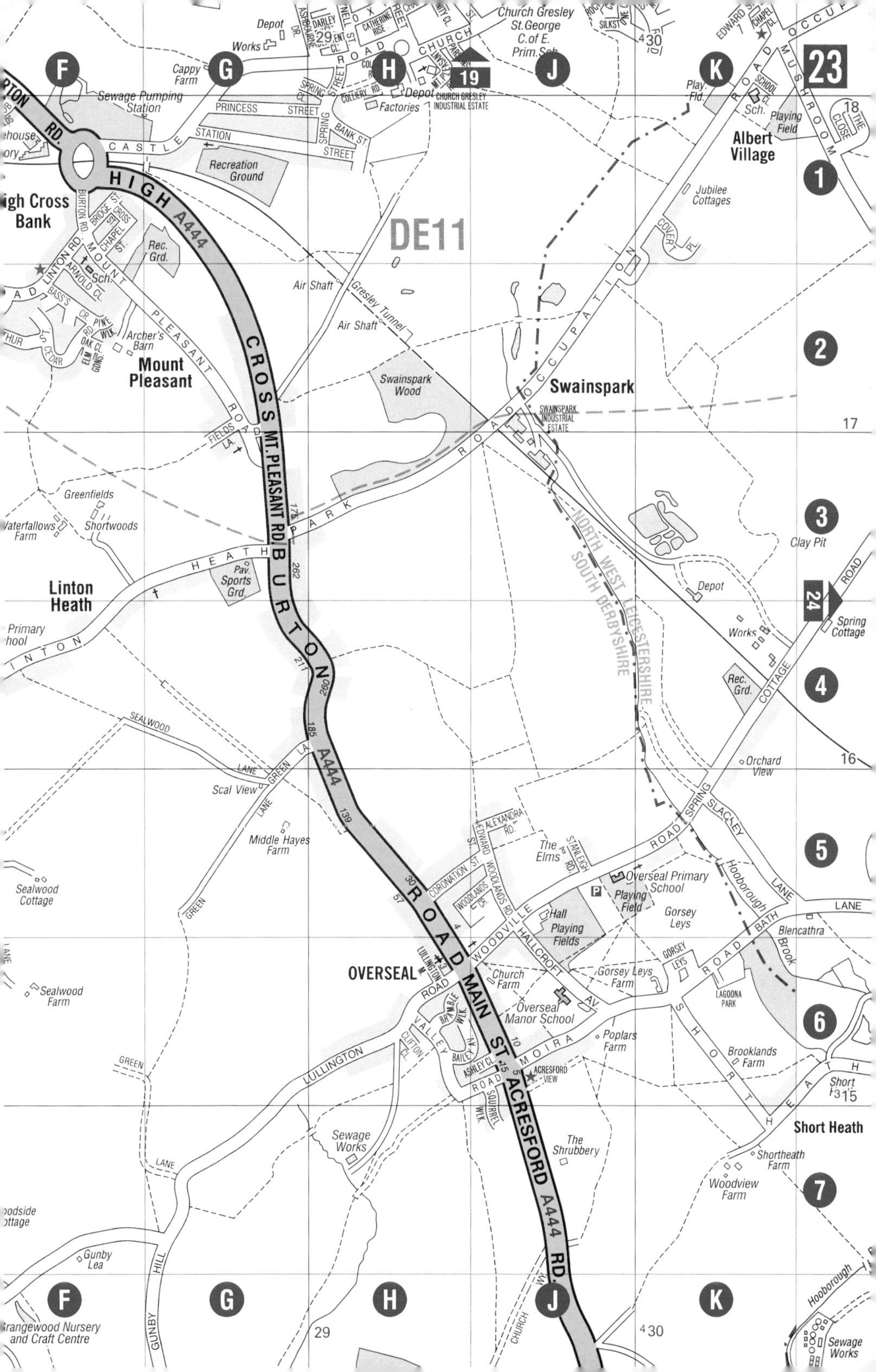
Church Gresley
St.George
C.of E.
Prim.Sch.
Depot
Works
Cappy Farm
Sewage Pumping Station
PRINCESS STREET
STATION STREET
CASTLE
Recreation Ground
Factories
CHURCH GRESLEY INDUSTRIAL ESTATE
19
Albert Village
Playing Field
Jubilee Cottages
High Cross Bank
HIGH A444
Rec. Grd.
DE11
Air Shaft
Gresley Tunnel
Archer's Barn
Mount Pleasant
Swainspark Wood
Swainspark
SWAINSPARK INDUSTRIAL ESTATE
OCCUPATION ROAD
CROSS
MT.PLEASANT RD.
BURTON
PARK ROAD
HEATH
Greenfields
Waterfallows Farm
Shortwoods
Pav. Sports Grd.
Linton Heath
LINTON
NORTH WEST LEICESTERSHIRE
SOUTH DERBYSHIRE
Clay Pit
Depot
24
Spring Cottage
Works
Rec. Grd.
COTTAGE
SEALWOOD LANE
GREEN LANE
Scal View
Middle Hayes Farm
A444
Orchard View
SPRING ROAD
SLACKEY LANE
The Elms
Overseal Primary School
Playing Field
Gorsey Leys
Hall Playing Fields
Sealwood Cottage
ROAD
OVERSEAL
WOODVILLE
HALLCROFT AV.
Church Farm
Gorsey Leys Farm
Blencathra
Brook
BATH ROAD
LAGOONA PARK
Overseal Manor School
MAIN ST.
MOIRA ROAD
Poplars Farm
Sealwood Farm
Brooklands Farm
LULLINGTON ROAD
ACRESFORD VIEW
Short Heath
Sewage Works
The Shrubbery
ACRESFORD A444 RD.
Shortheath Farm
Woodview Farm
Gunby Lea
GUNBY HILL
Grangewood Nursery and Craft Centre
CHURCH
Hooborough
Sewage Works
F G H J K
1 2 3 4 5 6 7
29
30
17
16
15

24
20
23
30
DE11
DE12
LITTLEWORTH
BOOTHORPE
Boothorpe Farm
Boothorpe Hall
Norrishill Farm
The Furlongs
Works
Cricket Ground
Drift Farm
Drift House
Moira Inf. Sch.
Norris Hill
Blackfordby C.of E. Prim. Sch.
Feanedock Covert
Hanging Hill
Hanginghill Farm
Rawdon Villas
Spring Cottage
Clay Pit
Sweethill Lodge
Community Centre
Opencast Workings
Factory
Picnic Site
Sarah's Wood
Depot
Heart of The National Forest Visitor Centre
The Woodlands
Office
Newfields
Newfield Farm
Football Ground
Moira
Blencathra
Hooborough
Cricket Ground
Playing Fld.
Mem.
FURNACE LANE INDUSTRIAL ESTATE
Warren House Farm
Furnace Plantation
Moira Furnace Museum
Recreation Grd.
Chapel Houses
Brooklands Farm
Short Heath
Shortheath Farm
Springfield Farm
Settling Tanks
Bramborough Farm
Fox Covert
Donisthorpe
Sewage Works
Donisthorpe Prim. Sch.
NORTH WEST
SOUTH
LEICESTERSHIRE
DERBYSHIRE
MOIRA ROAD
RESERVOIR LANE
RAWDON HILL
MEASHAM ROAD
SHORTHEATH ROAD
BLACKFORDBY LANE
WILLESLEY
BOOTHORPE LANE
GORSE LANE
COTTAGE ROAD
BATH LANE
FURNACE LANE
SCHOOL ST.
POPLAR AV.
IVANHOE WAY
DONISTHORPE
HILL STREET

Blackfordby Hall
Lady Wood
Annwell House
ANNWELL PLACE
21
Holywell Farm
The Bungalow
Works
Depot
TOURNAMENT WAY
IVANHOE INDUSTRIAL ESTATE
Dairy
Rosecrea
Newlands
Prestop Park Farm
Ingle Hill Farm
Blackfordby
Blackfordby Fields
Lynwood
Thorntop
Nursery
Ingle Bank
Ingle's Hill
Prestop Park
Holywell Spring Farm
BURTON
WESTMINSTER WAY
MILLFIELD CL.
KING GEORGE AV.
HOLYWELL AV.
CANTERBURY
WINCHESTER WY.
MARLBOROUGH WAY
CHURCHILL
HIGHFIELDS CL.
KILWARDBY
Cheatle's Barn
Lower Mead House
Whitehouse Farm
Shellbrook
MOIRA ROAD
Play. Fld.
Woodside Farm
Shellbrook Farm
Prim. Sch.
Cemetery
ASHBY-DE-LA-ZOUCH
TRINITY
WILFRED GDNS.
PITHIVIERS
HUNTINGDON RD.
WOODSIDE
STATION
LE65
IVANHOE WAY
GRANGE
LODGE CL.
GRIFFITH GDNS.
Ashby Ct. Nursing Home
TAMWORTH ROAD
AVENUE RD.
Western Park
Willesley Prim. Sch.
Club House
Valley Farm
Rotherwood
Wood Farm
The Limes
White Lodge
Weir
Works
WILLESLEY ROAD
Wood Farm Cottages
Hill Farm Cottage
Hill Farm
WILLESLEY PARK GOLF COURSE
MEASHAM ROAD
A42
The Spinney
(disused)
WILLESLEY PARK
Mon.
South Lodge
31
Sports Ground
Sewage Treatment
34
435
F G H J K
1 2 3 4 5 6 7
16 17 18 26

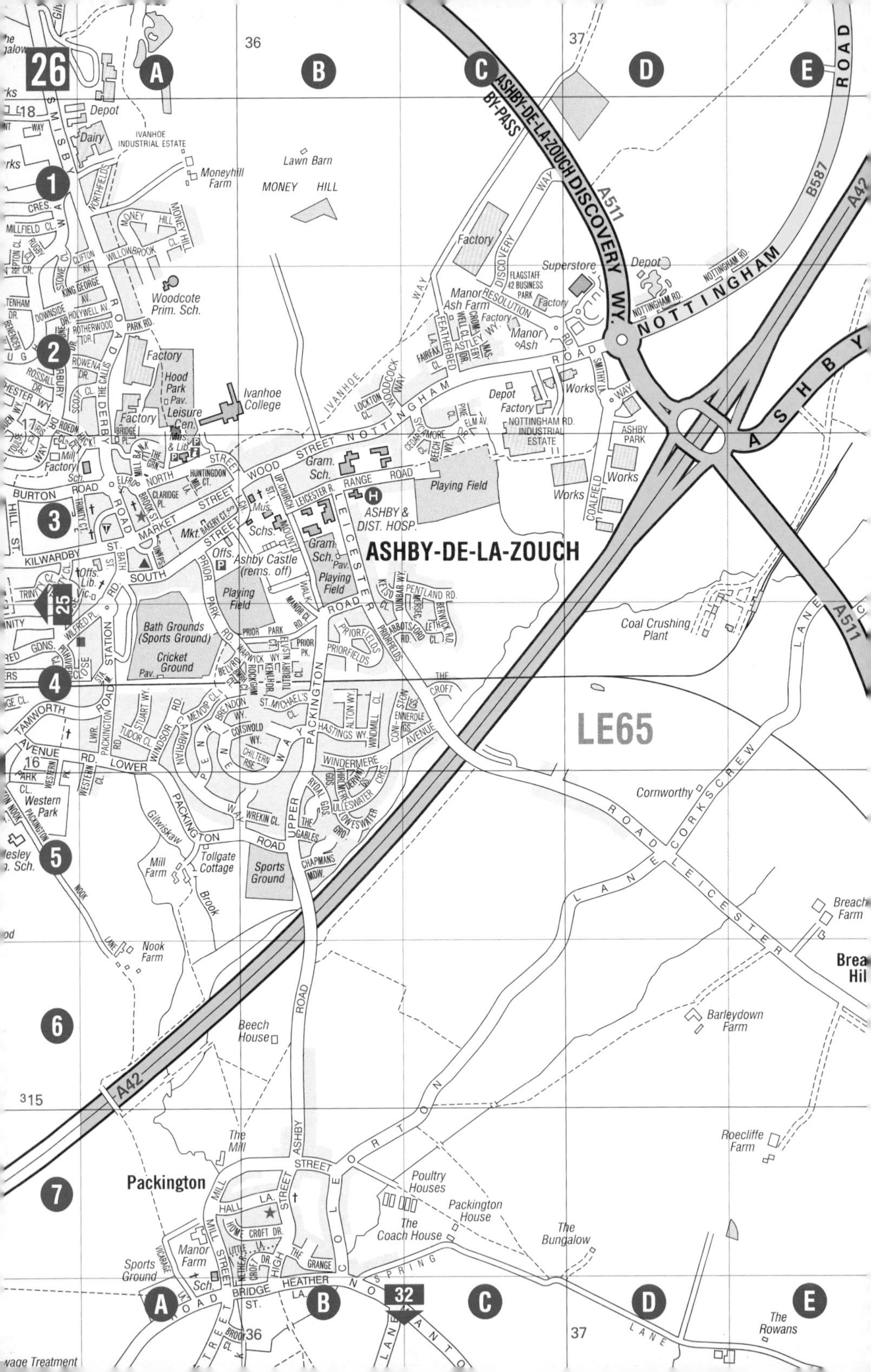

26
A
B
C
D
E
36
37
1
2
3
4
5
6
7
315
ASHBY-DE-LA-ZOUCH
LE65
Depot
Dairy
IVANHOE INDUSTRIAL ESTATE
Moneyhill Farm
Lawn Barn
MONEY HILL
Woodcote Prim. Sch.
Factory
Hood Park
Leisure Cen.
Ivanhoe College
Mus. & Lib.
Mill
Gram. Sch.
ASHBY & DIST. HOSP.
Playing Field
Mkt.
Offs.
Lib.
Vic.
Ashby Castle (rems. off)
Schs.
Pav.
Bath Grounds (Sports Ground)
Cricket Ground
Western Park
Wesley Sch.
Mill Farm
Tollgate Cottage
Sports Ground
Brook
Nook Farm
Beech House
The Mill
Packington
Manor Farm
Sch.
Poultry Houses
Packington House
The Coach House
The Bungalow
Roecliffe Farm
Barleydown Farm
Breach Farm
The Rowans
Cornworthy
Coal Crushing Plant
Works
ASHBY PARK
NOTTINGHAM RD. INDUSTRIAL ESTATE
Superstore
FLAGSTAFF 42 BUSINESS PARK
Manor Ash Farm
Manor Ash
ASHBY-DE-LA-ZOUCH BY-PASS
DISCOVERY WY.
A511
A42
B587
NOTTINGHAM ROAD
ASHBY ROAD
WOOD STREET
MARKET STREET
SOUTH STREET
BURTON ROAD
DERBY ROAD
STATION ROAD
TAMWORTH ROAD
LOWER PACKINGTON RD.
UPPER PACKINGTON ROAD
LEICESTER ROAD
CORKSCREW LANE
COLEORTON LANE
HEATHER LA.
BRIDGE ST.
ASHBY STREET
HIGH STREET
MILL STREET
HALL LA.
PRIOR PARK RD.
PENN WAY
SMISBY WAY
RANGE ROAD
IVANHOE WAY
32
25
Sewage Treatment

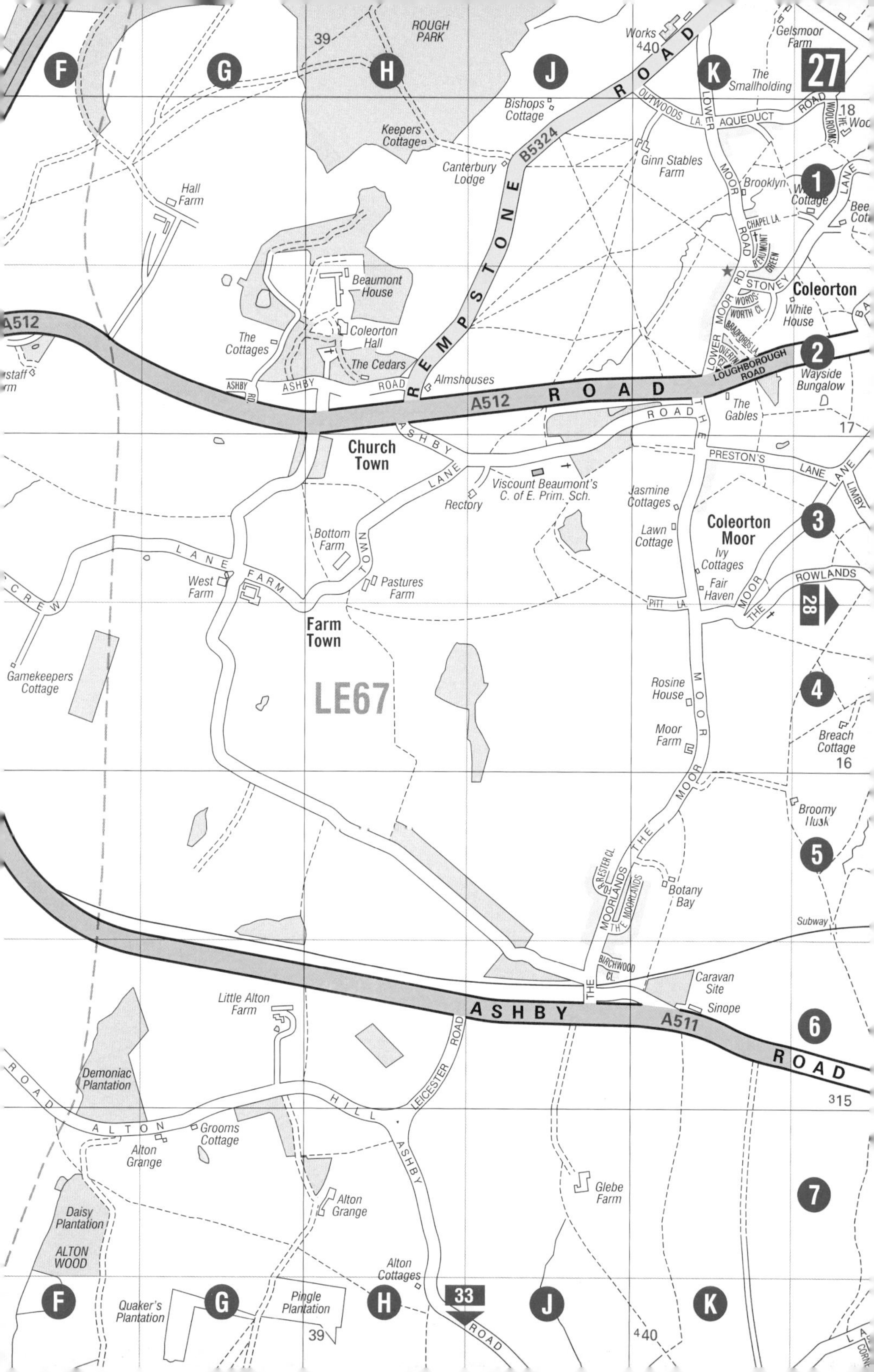

27
28
33
F
G
H
J
K
1
2
3
4
5
6
7
39
440
18
17
16
315
ROUGH PARK
Works
Gelsmoor Farm
The Smallholding
Bishops Cottage
Keepers Cottage
Canterbury Lodge
Ginn Stables Farm
Hall Farm
Brooklyn
Beaumont House
Coleorton Hall
The Cedars
The Cottages
Almshouses
Coleorton
White House
Wayside Bungalow
The Gables
Church Town
Viscount Beaumont's C. of E. Prim. Sch.
Rectory
Jasmine Cottages
Lawn Cottage
Coleorton Moor
Ivy Cottages
Fair Haven
Bottom Farm
Pastures Farm
West Farm
Farm Town
Gamekeepers Cottage
LE67
Rosine House
Moor Farm
Breach Cottage
Broomy Husk
Botany Bay
Subway
Caravan Site
Sinope
Little Alton Farm
Demoniac Plantation
Grooms Cottage
Alton Grange
Glebe Farm
Daisy Plantation
ALTON WOOD
Alton Cottages
Quaker's Plantation
Pingle Plantation
A512
B5324
A511
REMPSTONE ROAD
ASHBY ROAD
A512 ROAD
LOUGHBOROUGH ROAD
OUTWOODS LA.
AQUEDUCT ROAD
LOWER MOOR ROAD
CHAPEL LA.
BEAUMONT GREEN
STONEY
WORTH CL.
ASHBY LANE
THE ROAD
PRESTON'S LANE
LIMBY LANE
ROWLANDS
FARM LANE
FARM TOWN
CREW
PITT LA.
THE MOOR
MOORLANDS
THE MOORLANDS
BIRCHWOOD CL.
ASHBY A511 ROAD
LEICESTER ROAD
ALTON HILL ROAD
ASHBY ROAD

Coleorton
Peggs Green
Millhouse Estate
Swannington
New Swannington
Thornborough
COALVILLE
LE67
LOUGHBOROUGH ROAD
ASHBY RD.
A512
ASHBY ROAD A511
STEPHENSON
SWANNINGTON RD.
A447
Swannington Towermill
Swannington Common
Highfield House
Pumping Station
Redhill Bungalow
Redhill Farm
RED HILL
School Lane Farm
Limby Hall
Cuckoo Gap Farm
Breach Cottage
Broomy Husk
Swannington Heritage Trail
Willow Tree Farm
Deepdale
Old Colliery House
Golf Course
Industrial Estate
STEPHENSON INDUSTRIAL ESTATE
THE HERMITAGE INDUSTRIAL ESTATE
Hoo Ash Farm
All Saints C.of E. Prim. Sch.
Swannington C. of E. Prim. Sch.
New Swannington Primary Sch.
Thringstone Prim Sch.
Football Grd.
Talbot House Farm
Mill Farm
Field House Farm
Cinder Hill
Vicarage
Gelsmoor Farm
The Poplars
Rose Cott
Brooklands
Hillcrest
Miners' Institute
Sunny Dene
Veleta
Anchor Farm
Lawn Villa
California Cottage
Willow Cottage
Beehive Cottage
White House
Wayside Bungalow
Woolrooms
Brookdale
Snibston Discovery Park
Colliery Trail
Exhib.Hall & Mus.
Bus Depot
34
27

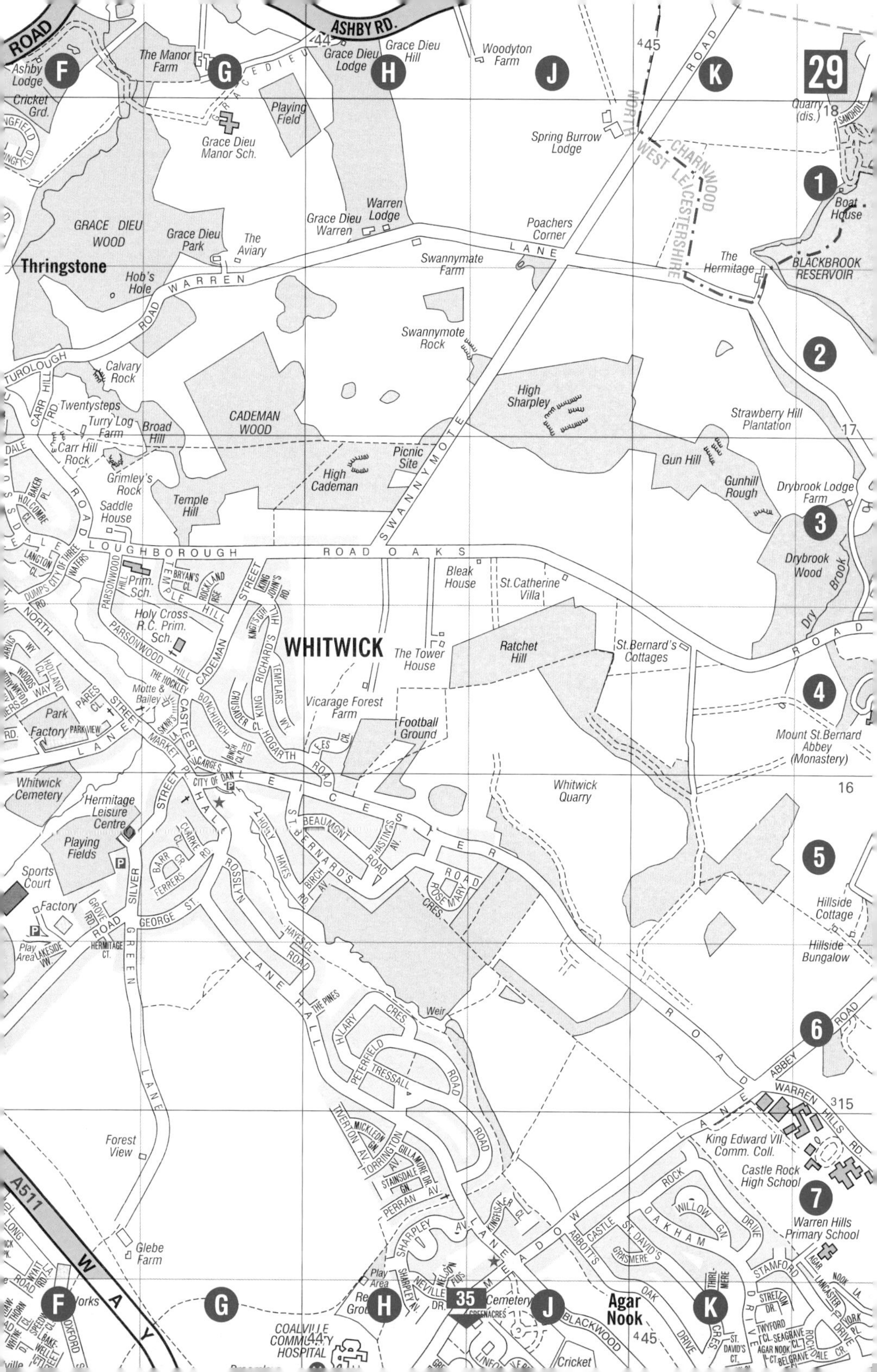
ASHBY RD.
ROAD
Ashby Lodge
Cricket Grd.
The Manor Farm
GRACE DIEU
Grace Dieu Lodge
Grace Dieu Hill
Woodyton Farm
Playing Field
Grace Dieu Manor Sch.
Spring Burrow Lodge
NORTH ROAD
CHARNWOOD
NORTH WEST LEICESTERSHIRE
Quarry (dis.)
SANDHOLE
Boat House
GRACE DIEU WOOD
Grace Dieu Park
The Aviary
Grace Dieu Warren
Warren Lodge
Poachers Corner
The Hermitage
BLACKBROOK RESERVOIR
Thringstone
Hob's Hole
WARREN LANE
Swannymate Farm
Swannymote Rock
TUROLOUGH
Calvary Rock
CARR HILL RD
Twentysteps
Turry Log Farm
Broad Hill
CADEMAN WOOD
High Sharpley
Strawberry Hill Plantation
Carr Hill Rock
Grimley's Rock
High Cademan
Picnic Site
SWANNYMOTE
Gun Hill
Gunhill Rough
Drybrook Lodge Farm
BAKER PL.
HOLCOMBE CL.
Saddle House
Temple Hill
Drybrook Wood
Dry Brook
LOUGHBOROUGH ROAD
OAKS ROAD
LANGTON CL.
CITY OF THREE WATERS
DUMPS RD.
PARSONWOOD HILL
Prim. Sch.
BRYAN'S CL.
ROCKLAND RSE.
TEMPLE HILL
KING JOHN'S RD.
Bleak House
St.Catherine Villa
Holy Cross R.C. Prim. Sch.
CADEMAN STREET
WHITWICK
The Tower House
Ratchet Hill
St.Bernard's Cottages
NORTH STREET
HOLLAND WAY
WOODS
PARES CL.
Park Factory
PARK VIEW
THE HOCKLEY
Motte & Bailey
KING RICHARD'S HILL
TEMPLARS' WY.
CRUSADER CL.
BONCHURCH RD
HOGARTH
Vicarage Forest Farm
Football Ground
Mount St.Bernard Abbey (Monastery)
Whitwick Quarry
CASTLE ST.
MARKET PL.
LEICESTER ROAD
Whitwick Cemetery
CITY OF DAN
Hermitage Leisure Centre
HALL
HOLLY HAYES
ST. BERNARD'S ROAD
BEAUMONT
HASTINGS AV.
ROSE MARY CRES.
Playing Fields
BARR CR.
CLARKE RD
FERRERS
ROSSLYN
BIRCH AV.
Sports Court
Factory
SILVER STREET
GROVE RD.
GEORGE ST.
Hillside Cottage
Hillside Bungalow
Play Area
LAKESIDE VW.
HERMITAGE CT.
GREEN LANE
HAYES CL.
HALL LANE
THE PINES
Weir
HILARY CRES.
PETERFIELD
TRESSALL ROAD
ABBEY ROAD
WARREN HILLS RD.
King Edward VII Comm. Coll.
Castle Rock High School
Warren Hills Primary School
Forest View
TIVERTON AV.
MICKLEDON GN.
TORRINGTON AV.
GILLAMOORE DR.
STAINSDALE GN.
PERRAN AV.
KINGFISHER CL.
MEADOW LANE
CASTLE ROCK DRIVE
WILLOW GN.
OAKHAM
ST. DAVID'S
GRASMERE
ABBOTT'S OAK DRIVE
A511
WAY
Glebe Farm
SHARPLEY AV.
NEVILLE DR.
Play Area
Cemetery
THIRLMERE CRES.
STAMFORD DRIVE
STRETTON DR.
AGAR NOOK LA.
LANCASTER
YORK PL.
TWYFORD CL.
SEAGRAVE CL.
AGAR NOOK CT.
BELGRAVE CT.
ROCHDALE CR.
Agar Nook
BLACKWOOD
Works
COALVILLE COMMUNITY HOSPITAL
Cricket
GREENACRES
OXFORD
35
F G H J K
1 2 3 4 5 6 7
18 17 16 315
444 445

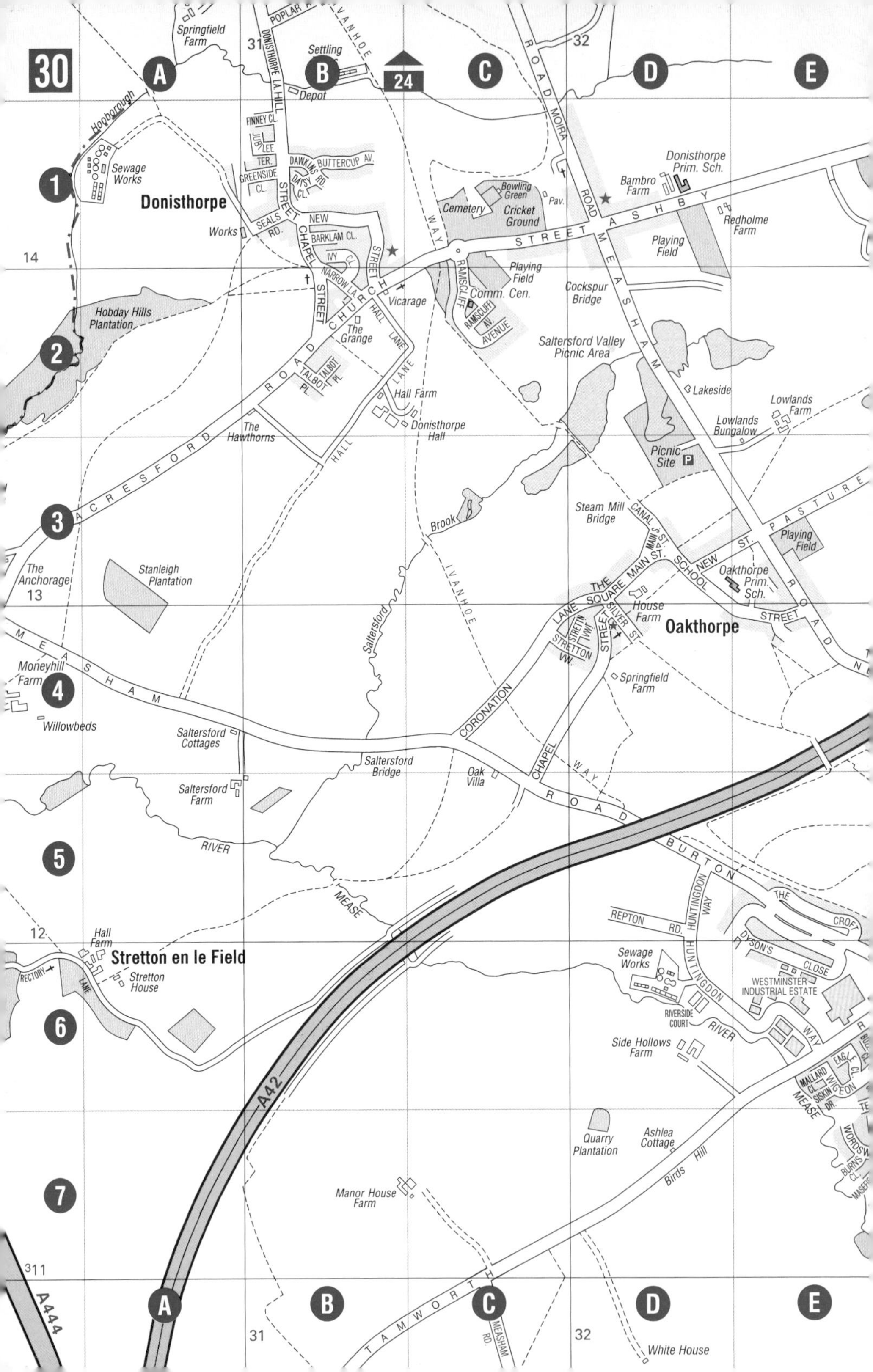
24
Donisthorpe
Oakthorpe
Stretton en le Field
Springfield Farm
Settling
Depot
Hooborough
Sewage Works
Works
Donisthorpe Prim. Sch.
Bambro Farm
Redholme Farm
Playing Field
Cemetery
Bowling Green
Cricket Ground
Pav.
Playing Field
Comm. Cen.
Vicarage
The Grange
Hall Farm
Donisthorpe Hall
The Hawthorns
Hobday Hills Plantation
Cockspur Bridge
Saltersford Valley Picnic Area
Lakeside
Lowlands Farm
Lowlands Bungalow
Picnic Site
Steam Mill Bridge
Playing Field
Oakthorpe Prim. Sch.
House Farm
Springfield Farm
Brook
Saltersford
Stanleigh Plantation
The Anchorage
Moneyhill Farm
Willowbeds
Saltersford Cottages
Saltersford Bridge
Saltersford Farm
Oak Villa
RIVER
MEASE
Hall Farm
Stretton House
Sewage Works
WESTMINSTER INDUSTRIAL ESTATE
RIVERSIDE COURT
Side Hollows Farm
Quarry Plantation
Ashlea Cottage
Birds Hill
Manor House Farm
White House
A42
A444
MOIRA ROAD
ASHBY STREET
MEASHAM ROAD
ACRESFORD ROAD
CHURCH STREET
CHAPEL STREET
NEW STREET
DONISTHORPE LA. HILL
POPLAR
IVANHOE WAY
FINNEY CL.
JUBILEE TER.
GREENSIDE CL.
SEALS RD.
DAWKINS RD.
DAISY CL.
BUTTERCUP AV.
BARKLAM CL.
IVY CL.
NARROW LA.
HALL LANE
TALBOT PL.
RAMSCLIFF AVENUE
RAMSCLIFF AV.
PASTURE
CANAL ST.
MAIN ST.
SCHOOL ST.
NEW ST.
THE SQUARE
LANE
STRETTON VW.
SILVER ST.
CHAPEL STREET
CORONATION
BURTON ROAD
REPTON RD.
HUNTINGDON WAY
THE CROFT
DYSON'S CLOSE
RIVER
MALLARD CL.
SISKIN DR.
WIGEON
MEASE
BURNS CL.
RECTORY LANE
TAMWORTH
MEASHAM RD.
A
B
C
D
E
1
2
3
4
5
6
7
14
13
12
311
31
32

31
Hill Farm
WILLESLEY PARK
South Lodge
Saltersford Brook
LE65
DE12
A42
MEASHAM RD.
B4116
Sweethill Cottage
Park Farm
WILLESLEY WOODSIDE
Reservoir (covered)
Brickfield Plantation
Pasture Farm
Field Farm Cottages
Field Farm
Emscote
The Firs
Spring Hydro (Health Farm)
Arlick Farm
Measham House Cottage
Measham House Farm
Fields Farm
Sewage Treatment Works
BABELAKE STREET
MEASHAM LANE
ASHBY ROAD
LEICESTER ROAD
BOSWORTH ROAD
SWEPSTONE ROAD
GALLOWS LANE
St. Charles' R. C. Prim. Sch.
Prim. Sch.
Recreation Ground
Nursery
Cemetery
The Bungalow
Ivyleigh
Measham Fields Farm
Stanhope House
Measham Hall
Depot
MEASHAM
Mus.
Vic.
Mem.
Ibstock Cottages
Works
Measham Lodge
Coronet House
Gilwiskaw Brook
The Spinney
Mon.
25
32

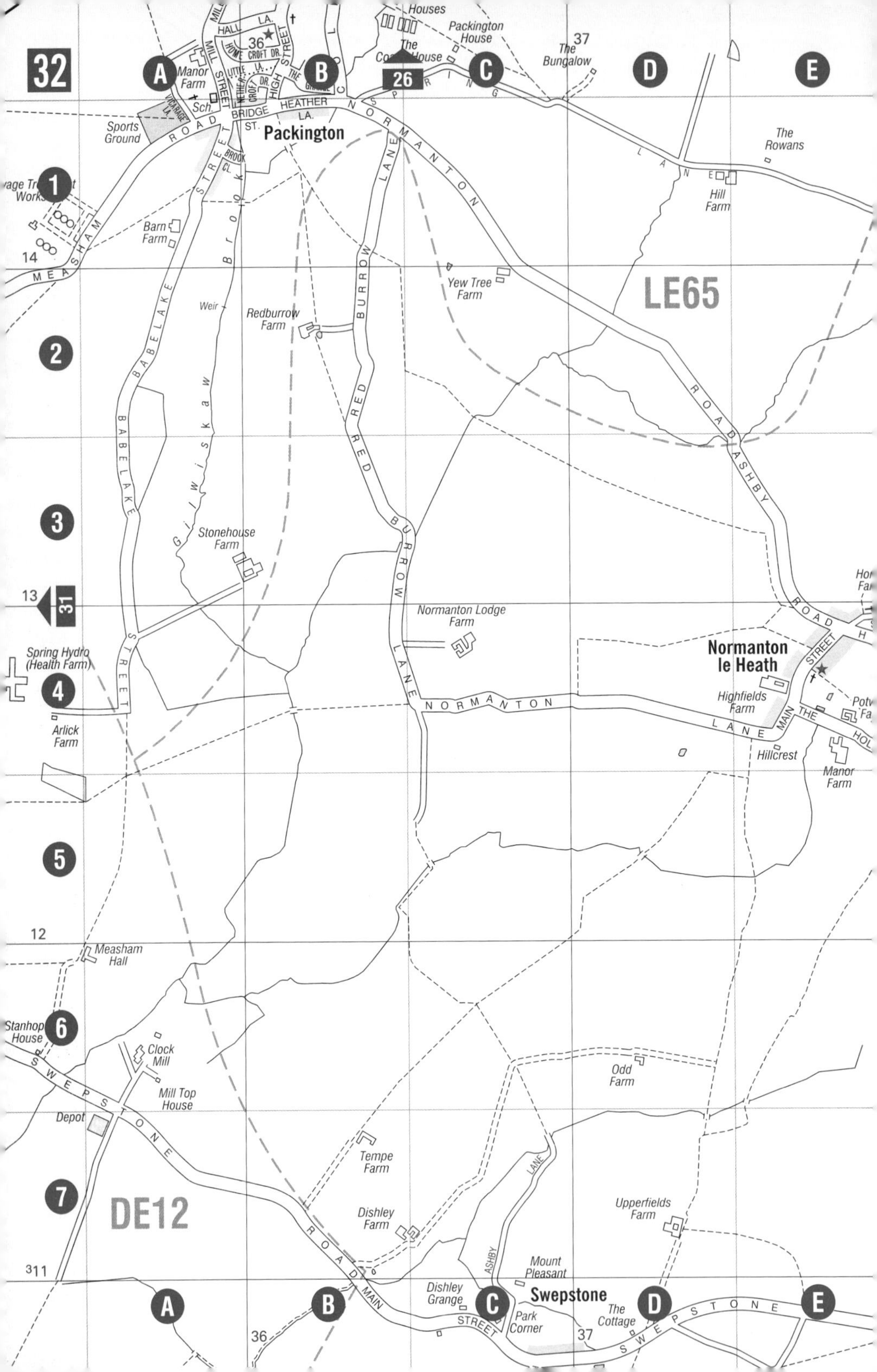
Packington
Normanton le Heath
Swepstone
LE65
DE12
Manor Farm
Sports Ground
Sch.
Houses
Packington House
The Coach House
26
The Bungalow
The Rowans
Hill Farm
Barn Farm
Weir
Redburrow Farm
Yew Tree Farm
Stonehouse Farm
Normanton Lodge Farm
Spring Hydro (Health Farm)
Arlick Farm
Highfields Farm
Hillcrest
Manor Farm
Measham Hall
Stanhope House
Clock Mill
Mill Top House
Depot
Odd Farm
Tempe Farm
Dishley Farm
Upperfields Farm
Mount Pleasant
Dishley Grange
Park Corner
The Cottage
31
HEATHER LA.
BRIDGE ST.
MILL STREET
HIGH STREET
HOME CROFT DR.
LITTLE LA.
VICARAGE LA.
BROOK CL.
MEASHAM ROAD
NORMANTON LANE
SPRING LANE
BABELAKE STREET
RED BURROW LANE
ASHBY ROAD
MAIN STREET
SWEPSTONE ROAD
ASHBY LANE
Gilwiskaw Brook
A
B
C
D
E
1
2
3
4
5
6
7
36
37
14
13
12
311

33
Daisy Plantation
Alton Grange
Glebe Farm
ALTON WOOD
Quaker's Plantation
Pingle Plantation
Alton Cottages
Spring Wood
The Altons
Ross Knob Plantation
Jubilee Plantation
Normanton Wood
Ravenstone Hall
Church Lane Fm.
Ravenstone Prim. Sch.
Tennis Cts.
Sports Pav. Field
Hall Farm
Ravenstone
Home Farm
Hall
Long Moor Spinney
Assage Wood
Sewage Works
Long Moor Farm
Hall Farm
LE67
Kelham Bridge Farm
OPENCAST WORKINGS
Thorntree Farm
Coal Disposal Point Plant
Cattows Farm
Heather St. John Sports & Social Club
Heather
Prim. Sch.
Works
Sparkenhoe Estate
Playing Field
INSET Page 34
ASHBY ROAD
CHURCH LANE
PIPER LANE
MAIN STREET
LEICESTER ROAD
JENNY'S LA.
MELBOURNE ROAD
A447
RAVENSTONE RD.
RAVENSTONE ROAD
HEATHER LANE
NORMANTON LANE
PISCA LANE
Blower's Brook
PENISTON
WINCHESTER CT.
ALBERT ST.
ARGYLE
27
34

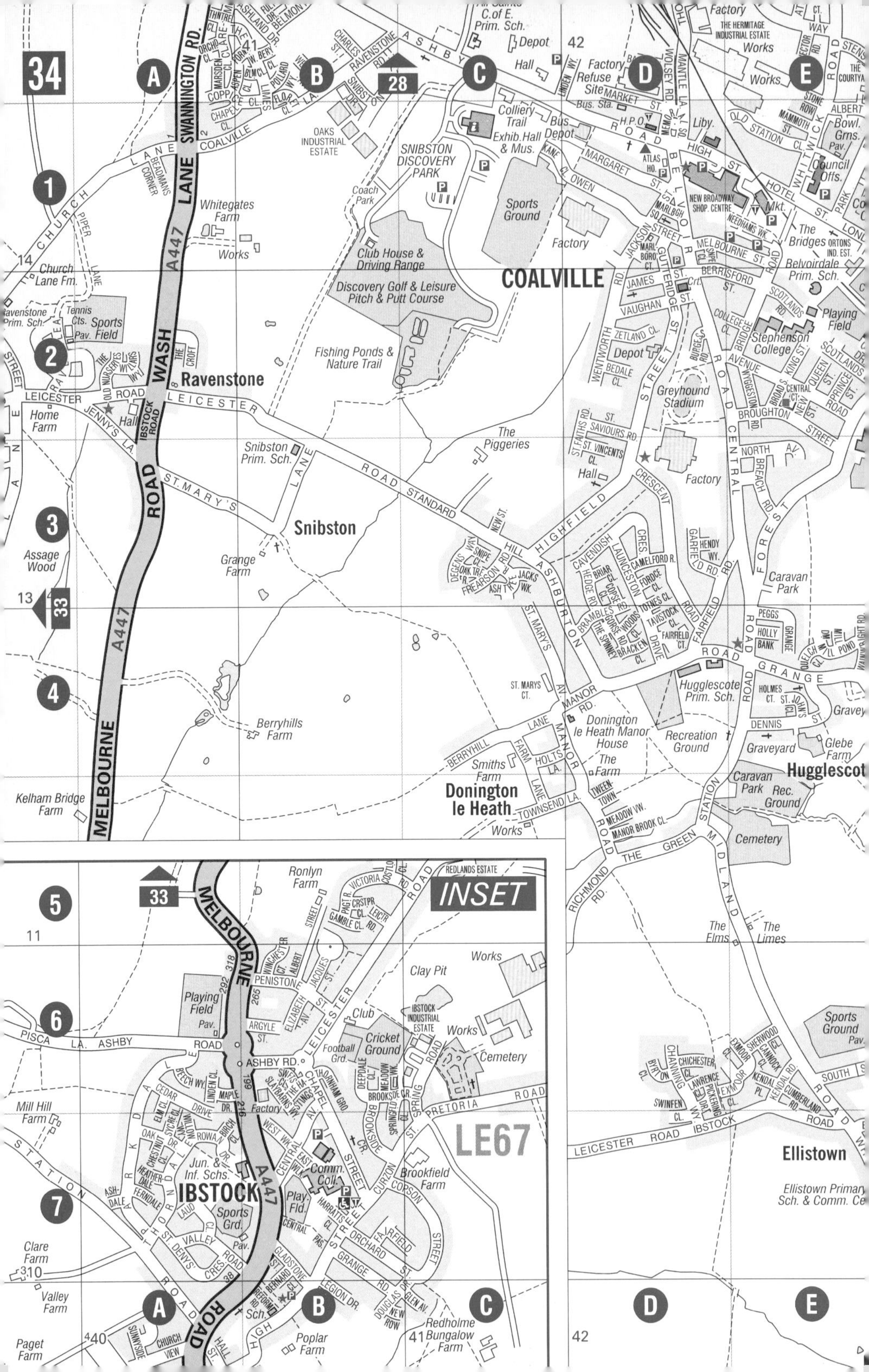

COALVILLE
Ravenstone
Snibston
Donington
le Heath
Hugglescot
Ellistown
IBSTOCK
INSET
LE67
SWANNINGTON RD.
WASH LANE
ROAD
MELBOURNE
A447
COALVILLE LANE
CHURCH LANE
LEICESTER ROAD
STANDARD HILL
ASHBURTON ROAD
HIGHFIELD ST.
BELVOIR ROAD
CENTRAL ROAD
FOREST ROAD
GRANGE ROAD
STATION ROAD
MIDLAND ROAD
LEICESTER ROAD
IBSTOCK ROAD
ASHBY ROAD
PISCA LA.
Whitegates Farm
Works
Church Lane Fm.
Ravenstone Prim. Sch.
Tennis Cts.
Sports Field
Pav.
Home Farm
Hall
Assage Wood
Kelham Bridge Farm
Snibston Prim. Sch.
Grange Farm
Berryhills Farm
OAKS INDUSTRIAL ESTATE
SNIBSTON DISCOVERY PARK
Coach Park
Colliery Trail
Exhib. Hall & Mus.
Club House & Driving Range
Discovery Golf & Leisure Pitch & Putt Course
Fishing Ponds & Nature Trail
The Piggeries
Sports Ground
Factory
Bus Depot
Refuse Site
Depot
Bus. Sta.
Liby.
NEW BROADWAY SHOP. CENTRE
Mkt.
Council Offs.
Bowl. Grns.
The Bridges
Belvoirdale Prim. Sch.
Stephenson College
Playing Field
Greyhound Stadium
Caravan Park
Hugglescote Prim. Sch.
Recreation Ground
Graveyard
Glebe Farm
Rec. Ground
Cemetery
Donington le Heath Manor House
The Farm
Smiths Farm
The Elms
The Limes
Sports Ground
Ellistown Primary Sch. & Comm. Ce
Ronlyn Farm
Clay Pit
IBSTOCK INDUSTRIAL ESTATE
Cricket Ground
Football Grd.
Cemetery
Playing Field
Mill Hill Farm
Jun. & Inf. Schs.
Sports Grd.
Comm. Coll.
Play. Fld.
Brookfield Farm
Clare Farm
Valley Farm
Paget Farm
Poplar Farm
Redholme Bungalow Farm
A
B
C
D
E
1
2
3
4
5
6
7
28
33
41
42
14
13
11
10
40

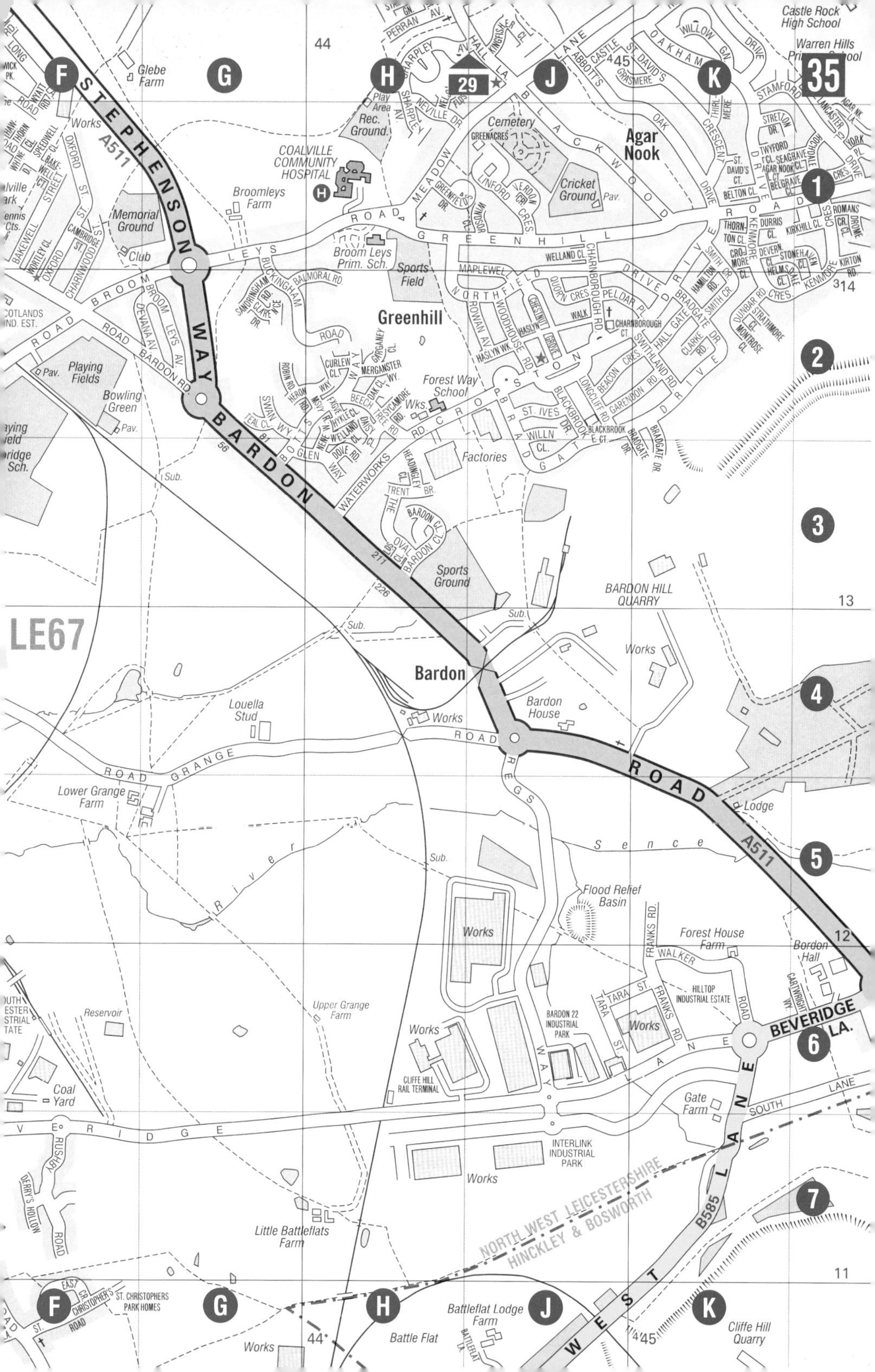

35
Castle Rock High School
Warren Hills Primary School
Agar Nook
COALVILLE COMMUNITY HOSPITAL
Broomleys Farm
Glebe Farm
Memorial Ground
Rec. Ground
Cemetery
Cricket Ground
Broom Leys Prim. Sch.
Sports Field
Greenhill
Forest Way School
Factories
Playing Fields
Bowling Green
Sports Ground
BARDON HILL QUARRY
Bardon
Bardon House
Louella Stud
Lower Grange Farm
Flood Relief Basin
Forest House Farm
Bordon Hall
HILLTOP INDUSTRIAL ESTATE
BARDON 22 INDUSTRIAL PARK
CLIFFE HILL RAIL TERMINAL
INTERLINK INDUSTRIAL PARK
Upper Grange Farm
Reservoir
Coal Yard
Little Battleflats Farm
Battleflat Lodge Farm
Battle Flat
Cliffe Hill Quarry
Gate Farm
ST. CHRISTOPHERS PARK HOMES
NORTH WEST LEICESTERSHIRE
HINCKLEY & BOSWORTH
LE67
STEPHENSON WAY
A511
BARDON ROAD
BEVERIDGE LA.
SOUTH LANE
WEST LANE
B585
GRANGE ROAD
GREENHILL ROAD
LEYS ROAD
BLACKWOOD
River Sence
REGS WAY
WATERWORKS RD.
CROPSTON DRIVE

INDEX

Including Streets, Hospitals & Hospices, Industrial Estates,
Selected Flats & Walkways and Selected Places of Interest.

HOW TO USE THIS INDEX

1. Each street name is followed by its Posttown or Postal Locality and then by its map reference; e.g. Abbey Dri. *Ash Z* . . . . 3J **25** is in the Ashby-de-la-Zouch Posttown and is to be found in square 3J on page **25.** The page number being shown in bold type.

2. A strict alphabetical order is followed in which Av., Rd., St., etc. (though abbreviated) are read in full and as part of the street name; e.g. Ashdale Clo. appears after Ash Dale but before Ash Dri.

3. Streets and a selection of flats and walkways too small to be shown on the maps, appear in the index in *Italics* with the thoroughfare to which it is connected shown in brackets; e.g. *Albion Ter. Burt T . . . . 1K **13** (off Derby Rd.)*

4. An example of a selected place of interest is **Ashby Castle. . . . 3B 26 (Remains of)**

5. An example of a hospital or hospice is **ASHBY & DISTRICT HOSPITAL. 3B 26**

GENERAL ABBREVIATIONS

All : Alley
App : Approach
Arc : Arcade
Av : Avenue
Bk : Back
Boulevd : Boulevard
Bri : Bridge
B'way : Broadway
Bldgs : Buildings
Bus : Business
Cvn : Caravan
Cen : Centre
Chu : Church
Chyd : Churchyard
Circ : Circle
Cir : Circus
Clo : Close
Comn : Common
Cotts : Cottages
Ct : Court
Cres : Crescent
Cft : Croft
Dri : Drive
E : East
Embkmt : Embankment
Est : Estate
Fld : Field
Gdns : Gardens
Gth : Garth
Ga : Gate
Gt : Great
Grn : Green
Gro : Grove
Ho : House
Ind : Industrial
Info : Information
Junct : Junction
La : Lane
Lit : Little
Lwr : Lower
Mc : Mac
Mnr : Manor
Mans : Mansions
Mkt : Market
Mdw : Meadow
M : Mews
Mt : Mount
Mus : Museum
N : North
Pal : Palace
Pde : Parade
Pk : Park
Pas : Passage
Pl : Place
Quad : Quadrant
Res : Residential
Ri : Rise
Rd : Road
Shop : Shopping
S : South
Sq : Square
Sta : Station
St : Street
Ter : Terrace
Trad : Trading
Up : Upper
Va : Vale
Vw : View
Vs : Villas
Vis : Visitors
Wlk : Walk
W : West
Yd : Yard

POSTTOWN AND POSTAL LOCALITY ABBREVIATIONS

A'lw : Anslow
Alb V : Albert Village
Ash Z : Ashby-de-la-Zouch
B'dby : Blackfordby
B'dry : Boundary
Bar H : Bardon Hill
Bar N : Barton under Needwood
Boo : Boothorpe
Bran : Branston
Bret : Bretby
Bur T : Burton-on-Trent
Burna : Burnaston
C'wll : Caldwell
Cas G : Castle Gresley
Chur B : Church Broughton
Chur G : Church Gresley
Coal : Coalville
Cole : Coleorton
Cot E : Coton-in-the-Elms
Don H : Donington le Heath
Doni : Donisthorpe
Drake : Drakelow
Egg : Eggington
Elli : Ellistown
Etw : Etwall
Find : Findern
Fos : Foston
Grif : Griffydam
Harts : Hartshorne
Hatt : Hatton
Heat : Heather
Hilt : Hilton
Hug : Hugglescote
Ibs : Ibstock
L'tn : Linton
Mea : Measham
Mid : Midway
Moi : Moira
N Pack : New Packington
N'seal : Netherseal
Need : Needwood
Newh : Newhall
Newt S : Newton Solney
Norm H : Normanton le Heath
Oakt : Oakthorpe
Over : Overseal
Pack : Packington
R'stn : Ravenstone
Rep : Repton
Rol D : Rolleston-on-Dove
Shell : Shellbrook
Smis : Smisby
Snar : Snarestone
Stant : Stanton
Stape : Stapenhill
Stret : Stretton
Swad : Swadlincote
Swan : Swannington
Swep : Swepstone
Tat : Tatenhill
Thri : Thringstone
Tut : Tutbury
W'sley : Willesley
W'vle : Woodville
Walt T : Walton-on-Trent
Whit : Whitwick
Will : Willington

A

Abbey Arc. *Burt T* 5K **13**
Abbey Clo. *Ash Z* 3J **25**
Abbey Dri. *Ash Z* 3J **25**
Abbey Lodge Clo. *Newh* 1H **19**
Abbey Rd. *Coal* 6K **29**
Abbey St. *Burt T* 6J **13**
Abbotsford Rd. *Ash Z* 4B **26**
Abbotts Clo. *Newh* 2H **19**
Abbott's Oak Dri. *Coal* 7J **29**
Abbotts Rd. *Newh* 2H **19**
Abney Cres. *Mea* 6F **31**
Abney Dri. *Mea* 6F **31**
Abney Wlk. *Mea* 6F **31**
Acacia Av. *Mid* 1J **19**
Acresford Rd. *Doni* 3A **30**
Acresford Rd. *Over* 6J **23**
Acresford Vw. *Over* 6J **23**
Addie Rd. *Burt T* 1G **13**
Adelaide Cres. *Burt T* 5D **14**
Agar Nook Ct. *Coal* 1K **35**
Agar Nook La. *Coal* 7K **29**
Aintree Clo. *Bran* 1E **16**
Albert Rd. *Chur G* 6H **19**
Albert Rd. *Coal* 1E **34**

Albert St. *Burt T* 3H **13**
Albert St. *Ibs* 6B **34**
Albion Clo. *Moi* 5D **24**
Albion St. *W'vle* 6C **20**
Albion Ter. Burt T 1K **13**
(off Derby Rd.)
Alderbrook Clo. *Rol D* 2G **9**
Alder Gro. *Burt T* 1A **18**
Alders Brook. *Hilt* 4J **5**
Aldersley Clo. *Find* 4K **7**
Alexandra Ct. *Burt T* 4B **14**
Alexandra Rd. *Burt T* 4B **14**
Alexandra Rd. *Over* 5J **23**
Alexandra Rd. *Swad* 5J **19**
Alfred St. *Burt T* 5H **13**
Allison Av. *Swad* 5J **19**
All Saints Cft. *Burt T* 7H **13**
All Saints Rd. *Burt T* 6G **13**
Alma Rd. *Newh* 2G **19**
Alma St. *Burt T* 5H **13**
Almond Ct. *Stret* 5K **9**
Almond Gro. *Newh* 3H **19**
Almshouses. *Etw* 1C **6**
Althorp Way. *Stret* 6J **9**
Alton Hill. *R'stn* 7F **27**
Alton Way. *Ash Z* 4B **26**
Amberlands. *Stret* 5A **10**
Amberwood. *Newh* 3H **19**
Amersham Way. *Mea* 4E **30**
Anchor La. *Cole* 1B **28**
Anderby Gdns. *Chur G* 6G **19**
Anderstaff Ind. Pk. *Burt T* 2J **13**
Anglesey Ct. *Burt T* 6G **13**
Anglesey Rd. *Burt T* 6G **13**
Anglesey St. *Burt T* 4E **12**
Annwell La. *Smis* 7H **21**
Anslow La. *Rol D* 4F **9**
Anson Ct. *Burt T* 4K **13**
Appleby Glade. *Cas G* 6E **18**
Appleby Glade Ind. Est. *Swad* 6F **19**
Appleton Clo. *Newh* 2G **19**
Appletree Rd. *Hatt* 4B **4**
Aqueduct Rd. *Cole* 1K **27**
Argyle St. *Ibs* 6B **34**
Arnold Clo. *Cas G* 2F **23**
Arnot Rd. *Bran* 7F **13**
Arnside Clo. *Chur G* 7K **19**
Arthurs Ct. *Stret* 4K **9**
Arthur St. *Burt T* 2H **13**
Arthur St. *Cas G* 2F **23**
Ascot Clo. *Burt T* 4B **14**
Ascott Dri. *Newh* 1H **19**
Ashbourne Dri. *Cas G* 7G **19**
Ashbrook. *Burt T* 6B **14**
Ashburton Rd. *Hug* 3C **34**
ASHBY & DISTRICT HOSPITAL. 3B 26
Ashby Castle. 3B 26
(Remains of)
Ashby-de-la-Zouch By-Pass.
B'dby & Ash Z 6G **21**
Ashby-de-la-Zouch Mus. & Library. 3A 26
Ashby La. *B'dby* 7F **21**
Ashby La. *Swep* 7C **32**
Ashby Pk. *Ash Z* 2D **26**
Ashby Rd. *Ash Z & Cole* 2E **26**
(in two parts)
Ashby Rd. *Burt T & Bret* 4A **14**
Ashby Rd. *Coal* 6J **27**
Ashby Rd. *Doni* 1D **30**
Ashby Rd. *Ibs* 6A **34**
(in two parts)
Ashby Rd. *Mea* 4G **31**
Ashby Rd. *Moi* 5C **24**
Ashby Rd. *Pack* 7B **26**
Ashby Rd. *R'stn* 7H **27**
Ashby Rd. *Thri* 1D **28**
Ashby Rd. *W'vle* 6D **20**
Ashby Rd. E. *Bret* 6F **15**
Ashdale. *Ibs* 7A **34**
Ash Dale. *Ibs* 2E **28**
Ashdale Clo. *Burt T* 7B **14**
Ash Dri. *Mea* 4F **31**
Ashfield Dri. *Moi* 3E **24**
Ashford Rd. *Burt T* 1F **13**
Ashford Rd. *Whit* 4E **28**
Ash Gro. La. *Egg* 7D **6**
Ashland Dri. *Coal* 7B **28**
Ash La. *Etw* 1B **6**
Ashleigh Av. *Newh* 3G **19**
Ashley Clo. *Burt T* 4B **14**
Ashley Clo. *Over* 6J **23**
Ashley Ct. *Burt T* 4B **14**
Ashover Rd. *Newh* 3F **19**
Ash St. *Burt T* 6G **13**
Ash Tree Clo. *Newh* 2G **19**
Ash Tree Rd. *Hug* 3C **34**
Ash Vw. Clo. *Etw* 1C **6**
Ashworth Av. *Burt T* 5D **14**
Askew Gro. *Rep* 4K **11**
Aspen Clo. *Mea* 4F **31**
Aspen Clo. *R'stn* 7B **28**
Aspens Hollow. *Thri* 2E **28**
Astil St. *Burt T* 6A **14**
Astley Way. *Ash Z* 2C **26**
Aston Dri. *Newh* 7H **15**
Atherstone Rd. *Mea* 6F **31**
Athlestan Way. *Stret* 4G **9**
Atkinson Rd. *Ash Z* 2J **25**
Atlas Ct. *Coal* 7E **28**
Atlas Ho. *Coal* 1D **34**
Atlas Rd. *Coal* 7E **28**
Audens Way. *Mid* 2K **19**
Aults Clo. *Find* 4K **7**
Avenue Rd. *Ash Z* 4K **25**
Avenue Rd. *Coal* 2E **34**
Averham Clo. *Swad* 5H **19**
Aviation La. *Burt T* 3B **12**
Avon Clo. *Swad* 2J **19**
Avon Way. *Burt T* 6B **14**
Avon Way. *Hilt* 4J **5**

B

Babbington Clo. *Tut* 1B **8**
Babelake St. *Pack* 2A **32**
Back La. *Hilt* 3H **5**
Bailey Av. *Over* 6H **23**
Bailey St. *Burt T* 6J **13**
Baker Av. *Ash Z* 4J **25**
Baker St. *Burt T* 1K **17**
Baker St. *Coal* 7D **28**
Baker St. *Swad* 5K **19**
Bakery Ct. *Ash Z* 3A **26**
Bakewell Ct. *Coal* 1F **35**
Bakewell Grn. *Newh* 3F **19**
Bakewells La. *Cole* 2A **28**
Bakewell St. *Coal* 1F **35**
Balfour St. *Burt T* 1H **13**
Balmoral Rd. *Burt T* 4B **14**
Balmoral Rd. *Coal* 2G **35**
Baltimore Clo. *Newh* 1H **19**
Bamborough Clo. *Stret* 7J **9**
Bamburgh Clo. *Ash Z* 4A **26**
Bancroft Clo. *Hilt* 3J **5**
Bancroft, The. *Etw* 1C **6**
Bank Passage. *Swad* 5J **19**
Bank St. *Cas G* 1H **23**
Bank Wlk. *Burt T* 6G **9**
Bardolph Clo. *Swad* 5G **19**
Bardon Clo. *Coal* 3H **35**
Bardon Rd. *Coal & Bar H* 2G **35**
Bardon 22 Ind. Pk. *Elli* 6J **35**
Bargate La. *Will* 1J **11**
Barklam Clo. *Doni* 1B **30**
Barley Clo. *Burt T* 1K **13**
Barleycorn Clo. *Burt T* 6B **14**
Barn Clo. *Find* 3K **7**
Barr Cres. *Whit* 5G **29**
Barrington Clo. *Stret* 5H **9**
Barton St. *Burt T* 7H **13**
Baslow Grn. *Newh* 3F **19**
Bass Cotts. *Burt T* 3K **13**
Bass Mus., The. 4J 13
Bass's Bldgs. *Burt T* 4G **13**
Bass's Cres. *Cas G* 2F **23**
Bath Grounds. 4A 26
(Sports Ground)
Bath La. *Moi* 5K **23**
Bath St. *Ash Z* 3A **26**
Battleflat La. *Elli* 7J **35**
Battlestead Hill Nature Reserve. 7B 12
Beacon Cres. *Coal* 2J **35**
Beacon Dri. *Rol D* 3G **9**
Beacon Rd. *Rol D* 4G **9**
Beaconsfield Rd. *Burt T* 7F **9**
Beadmans Corner. *R'stn* 1A **34**
Beam Clo. *Burt T* 6F **9**
Beamhill Rd. *A'lw & Burt T* 6D **8**
Beards Rd. *Newh* 2H **19**
Bearwood Hill Rd. *Burt T* 4A **14**
Beaufort Rd. *Burt T* 6B **14**
Beaumont Av. *Ash Z* 3J **25**
Beaumont Grn. *Cole* 1K **27**
Beaumont Rd. *Whit* 5H **29**
Becket Clo. *Burt T* 1G **13**
Bedale Clo. *Coal* 2D **34**
Bedford Rd. *Burt T* 1J **17**
Beech Av. *R'stn* 2K **33**
Beech Av. *Stret* 6A **10**
Beech Av. *Will* 1H **11**
Beech Dri. *Etw* 1D **6**
Beech Dri. *Stret* 6K **9**
Beech Dri. *W'vle* 6E **20**
Beech Gro. *Newh* 1G **19**
Beech La. *Stret* 5K **9**
(in two parts)
Beech St. *Burt T* 6G **13**
Beech Tree Rd. *Coal* 2H **35**
Beech Way. *Ash Z* 3C **26**
Beech Way. *Ibs* 6A **34**
Beehive Av. *Moi* 5D **24**
Bee Hives, The. *Newh* 1H **19**
Belcher Clo. *Heat* 7G **33**
Belfield Ct. *Etw* 2C **6**
Belfield Rd. *Etw* 2C **6**
Belfield Rd. *Swad* 4J **19**
Belfield Ter. *Etw* 2D **6**
Belfry, The. *Stret* 5H **9**
Belgrave Clo. *Coal* 1K **35**
Bell La. *Harts* 5D **20**
Bells End Rd. *Walt T* 7C **16**
Belmont Dri. *Coal* 7B **28**
Belmont St. *Swad* 4K **19**
Belmot Rd. *Need & Tut* 3A **8**
Belton Clo. *Coal* 1K **35**
Belvedere Rd. *Burt T* 1F **13**
Belvedere Rd. *W'vle* 6C **20**
Belvoir Clo. *Burt T* 2G **13**
Belvoir Cres. *Newh* 2H **19**
Belvoir Dri. *Ash Z* 4A **26**
Belvoir Rd. *Burt T* 2F **13**
Belvoir Rd. *Coal* 1D **34**
Bend Oak Dri. *Burt T* 3D **14**
Benenden Way. *Ash Z* 2K **25**
Bent La. *Chur B* 1B **4**
Bentley Brook. *Hilt* 4J **5**
Bentley Dale. *Harts* 5D **20**
Beowulf Covert. *Stret* 5G **9**
Beresford Dale. *Chur G* 6G **19**
Bernard Clo. *Ibs* 7B **34**
Bernard Ct. *W'vle* 5A **20**
Bernard St. *W'vle* 5A **20**
Berrisford St. *Coal* 2D **34**
Berry Clo. *R'stn* 7B **28**
Berry Gdns. *Burt T* 3D **14**
Berry Hedge La. *Burt T* 3D **14**
Berryhill La. *Don H* 4C **34**
Berwick Rd. *Ash Z* 4C **26**
Best Av. *Burt T & Stape* 6C **14**
Beveridge La. *Elli & Bar H* 7F **35**
Beverley Rd. *Bran* 1E **16**
Birch Av. *Newh* 1G **19**
Birch Av. *Whit* 5H **29**
Birch Clo. *Bran* 7F **13**
Birches Clo. *Stret* 6J **9**
Birchfield Rd. *Burt T* 2K **17**
Birch Gro. *Hatt* 3C **4**
Birchwood Clo. *Cole* 6J **27**
Birkdale Av. *Bran* 2F **17**
Bishop Dale. *Thri* 2E **28**
Bishops Ga. *W'vle* 6B **20**
Bitham Ct. *Stret* 5H **9**
Bitham La. *Stret* 5H **9**
Blackbrook Ct. *Coal* 2J **35**
Blackbrook Dri. *Coal* 2J **35**
Blackett Dri. *Heat* 7G **33**
Blackfordby La. *Moi* 2E **24**
Blackpool St. *Burt T* 7H **13**
Blacksmiths La. *Egg* 7B **6**
Blacksmiths La. *Newt S* 6F **11**

Blacksmith's La. *W'vle* 5C **20**
Blacksmiths Yd. *Rol D* 2G **9**
Blackthorn Rd. *Burt T* 2K **17**
Blackthorn Way. *Mea* 4F **31**
Blackwood. *Coal* 1J **35**
Bladon Houses. *Newt S* 1C **14**
Bladon St. *Burt T* 3D **14**
Bladon's Yd. *Rol D* 2G **9**
Bladon Vw. *Stret* 4A **10**
Blakelow Dri. *Etw* 2C **6**
Bleach Mill. *Mea* 7F **31**
Blenheim Clo. *Burt T* 4D **14**
Blenheim Clo. *Newh* 1H **19**
Blenheim M. *Etw* 1D **6**
Blithe Clo. *Hilt* 4K **5**
Bloom Clo. *R'stn* 7B **28**
Bloomfield Clo. *Hilt* 4J **5**
Blossom Wlk. *Hatt* 4B **4**
Bluestone La. *Burt T* 1A **18**
Blythfield. *Burt T* 3K **13**
Boardman Rd. *Swad* 5F **19**
Boardman's Ind. Est. *Swad* 5F **19**
Bonchurch Clo. *Whit* 4G **29**
Bonchurch Rd. *Whit* 4G **29**
Bond St. *Burt T* 6J **13**
Boot Hill. *Rep* 3K **11**
Boothorpe La. *Boo* 1D **24**
Booth Rd. *Thri* 1E **28**
Borough Rd. *Burt T* 4H **13**
Bosworth Dri. *Burt T* 1G **13**
Bosworth Rd. *Mea & Snar* 5F **31**
Botts Way. *Coal* 3G **35**
Boundary Rd. *Etw* 5D **6**
Bourne Clo. *Tut* 7A **4**
Bourne Way. *Swad* 4A **20**
Bowker Cres. *Ash Z* 4J **25**
Bracken Clo. *Hug* 4D **34**
Brackenwood Rd. *Burt T* 2K **17**
Bradfords La. *Cole* 2K **27**
Bradgate Dri. *Coal* 2K **35**
Bradley St. *Burt T* 1K **17**
Bradmore Rd. *Burt T* 2G **13**
Bradshaw Mdw. *Hatt* 3B **4**
Brailsford Av. *Newh* 3E **18**
Bramble Ct. *Burt T* 2K **17**
Brambles Rd. *Hug* 4D **34**
Bramble Wlk. *Over* 6H **23**
Bramell Clo. *Bran* 1E **16**
Bramley Ct. *Hatt* 4B **4**
Bramley Dale. *Chur G* 6G **19**
Branston Golf Course. 2G 17
Branston Rd. *Burt T* 7H **13**
Branston Rd. *Tat* 7A **12**
Branston Water Pk. 2B 16
Branston Water Pk. Vis. Cen. 1C 16
Breach La. *Fos* 2B **4**
Breach Rd. *Coal* 3E **34**
Breadsall Clo. *Newh* 1H **19**
Brendon Way. *Ash Z* 4A **26**
Bren Way. *Hilt* 3K **5**
Bretby Bus. Pk. *Bret* 7G **15**
Bretby La. *Bret* 5E **14**
Bretby M. *Bret* 5J **15**
Bretby Rd. *Newh* 2G **19**
Bretby Vw. *Harts* 4D **20**
Bretlands Way. *Burt T* 2B **18**
Brewhouse Art Cen., The. 5J 13
Briar Clo. *B'dby* 1E **24**
Briar Clo. *Hug* 3D **34**
Briar Clo. *Newh* 3G **19**
Brick Kiln La. *Rol D* 3F **9**
Bridge Clo. *Chur G* 6K **19**
Bridge Farm. *Stret* 5K **9**
Bridge M. *Whit* 6E **28**
Bridge Pl. *Ash Z* 2A **26**
Bridge Rd. *Coal* 2E **34**
Bridgeside. *Stret* 5K **9**
Bridge St. *Burt T* 4K **13**
Bridge St. *Cas G* 1F **23**
Bridge St. *Chur G* 6K **19**
Bridge St. *Pack* 1B **32**
Bridge St. *Stret* 5K **9**
Bridge St. *Tut* 6B **4**
Bridgford Av. *Bran* 1E **16**
Bridle La. *Stant* 4B **18**
(in two parts)
Bridle Rd. *Coal* 6D **28**
Briers Way. *Whit* 4F **29**
Bristol Av. *Ash Z* 5K **25**
Britannia Dri. *Stret* 6J **9**
Briton Lodge Clo. *Moi* 5C **24**
Brittany Av. *Ash Z* 2K **25**
Brizlincote La. *Bret* 6E **14**
Brizlincote St. *Burt T* 6A **14**
Broadlands. *Stret* 6J **9**
Broad St. *Coal* 2E **34**
Broadway St. *Burt T* 7H **13**
Broadway Vs. *Swad* 2H **19**
Bronte Clo. *Burt T* 7J **9**
Brook Clo. *Hatt* 3C **4**
Brook Clo. *Pack* 1A **32**
Brookdale Rd. *Harts* 4D **20**
Brook End. *Rep* 3K **11**
Brook Ho. M. *Newh* 1H **19**
Brook La. *Fos* 2B **4**
Brook La. *Thri* 2E **28**
Brook Side. Ash Z *3A* ***26***
(off Brook St.)
Brookside. *Burt T* 2C **14**
Brook Side. *Rol D* 2G **9**
Brookside Clo. *Rep* 4K **11**
Brookside Cres. *Ibs* 6B **34**
Brooks La. *Whit* 4E **28**
Brook St. *Ash Z* 3A **26**
Brook St. *Burt T* 3J **13**
Brook St. *Harts* 1D **20**
Brook St. *Newh* 2F **19**
Brook St. *Swad* 5H **19**
Broomhills La. *Rep* 5K **11**
Broom Leys Av. *Coal* 2G **35**
Broom Leys Rd. *Coal* 2F **35**
Brough Rd. *Burt T* 4D **14**
Broughton St. *Coal* 2E **34**
Brown Ct. *Ash Z* 2J **25**
Browning Dri. *Mea* 7E **30**
Browning Rd. *Swad* 3K **19**
Brunt's La. *Egg* 7D **6**
Bryan's Clo. *Whit* 3G **29**
Bryony. *Bran* 7G **13**
Buckingham Clo. *Stret* 6J **9**
Buckingham Ct. *Burt T* 4D **14**
Buckingham Rd. *Coal* 1G **35**
Buckley Clo. *Mea* 6F **31**
Buckley Clo. *W'vle* 6D **20**
Burgess Rd. *Coal* 2D **34**
Burnaston La. *Etw* 1D **6**
Burns Clo. *Mea* 7E **30**
Burnside. *Rol D* 3G **9**
Burrows, The. *Newh* 3G **19**
Burton Albion F.C. 1J 13
Burton Enterprise Pk. *Burt T* 1K **13**
Burton-on-Trent Golf Course. 6F 15
Burton Pl. Shop. Cen. *Burt T* 5J **13**
Burton Rd. *Ash Z* 7H **21**
Burton Rd. *Bran* 1F **17**
Burton Rd. *Bret & Mid* 7H **15**
(in two parts)
Burton Rd. *Cas G* 6E **18**
Burton Rd. *Egg & Find* 7F **7**
Burton Rd. *Mid & W'vle* 2A **20**
Burton Rd. *Oakt & Mea* 5D **30**
Burton Rd. *Over* 3G **23**
Burton Rd. *Rep* 5H **11**
Burton Rd. *Tut* 6C **4**
Burtons La. *Swan* 4B **28**
Burton St. *Tut* 7B **4**
Burton Upon Trent Bowling Alley. 4K 13
Bushton La. *Tut & A'lw* 4A **8**
Butler Ct. *Burt T* 4G **13**
Buttercup Av. *Doni* 1B **30**
Butt La. *W'vle & B'dry* 6D **20**
Buxton Clo. *Newh* 1H **19**
Buxton Pl. *Burt T* 5K **13**
Buzzard Clo. *Mea* 6E **30**
Byrkley St. *Burt T* 3G **13**
Byron Av. *Burt T* 1K **17**
Byron Cres. *Mea* 7F **31**
Byron Rd. *Swad* 2K **19**
Byrton Clo. *Elli* 6D **34**

C

Cademan St. *Whit* 4G **29**
Cadley Hill Ind. Est. *Swad* 6E **18**
Cadleyhill Rd. *Swad* 6E **18**
Caernarvon Clo. *Stret* 6J **9**
Cairns Clo. *Burt T* 4D **14**
Calais Rd. *Burt T* 1G **13**
Calder Clo. *Hilt* 4J **5**
Caldwell Rd. *C'wll* 3A **22**
Calgary Cres. *Burt T* 4E **14**
Callingwood La. *Tat* 5A **12**
Callis, The. *Ash Z* 2A **26**
Cambrian Way. *Ash Z* 4A **26**
Cambrian Way. *Swad* 5H **19**
Cambridge St. *Burt T* 6G **13**
Cambridge St. *Coal* 1F **35**
Camelford Rd. *Hug* 3D **34**
Camelot Clo. *Stret* 4K **9**
Cameron Clo. *Burt T* 6C **14**
Campion Rd. *W'vle* 4B **20**
Canal Bri. *Will* 7H **7**
Canal St. *Burt T* 5H **13**
Canal St. *Oakt* 3D **30**
Canner Clo. *W'vle* 6D **20**
Cannock Clo. *Elli* 6E **34**
Canterbury Dri. *Ash Z* 2K **25**
Canterbury Rd. *Burt T* 4D **14**
Caraway Dri. *Bran* 7F **13**
Carisbrooke Dri. *Stret* 5K **9**
Carlton Ct. Burt T *4G* ***13***
(off Shobnall Rd.)
Carlton St. *Burt T* 1G **13**
Caroline Ter. *Burt T* 5H **13**
Carousels, The. *Burt T* 2H **13**
Carpenter Clo. *Stape* 5D **14**
Carr Hill Rd. *Whit* 2F **29**
Carriers Rd. *Egg* 6D **6**
Carter Dale. *Whit* 3E **28**
Cartwright Way. *Bar H* 6K **35**
Carver Rd. *Burt T* 1G **13**
Casey La. *Burt T* 3G **13**
Castle Ct. *Tut* 6B **4**
Castle Hayes La. *Tut* 1A **8**
Castle Hill. *Find* 4K **7**
Castle M., The. *Newh* 1H **19**
Castle Pk. Rd. *Burt T* 7G **9**
Castle Rd. *Cas G* 1F **23**
Castle Rock Dri. *Coal* 7J **29**
Castle St. *Tut* 6A **4**
Castle St. *Whit* 4G **29**
Castle Vw. *Hatt* 5B **4**
Castle Way. *Ash Z* 5K **25**
Castleway, The. *Egg & Will* 7F **7**
Catherine Ri. *Chur G* 7H **19**
Cavendish Clo. *Newh* 1H **19**
Cavendish Cres. *Hug* 3D **34**
Cecil Rd. *Newh* 3G **19**
Cedar Clo. *Ash Z* 3C **26**
Cedar Dri. *Ibs* 6A **34**
Cedar Gro. *L'tn* 3D **22**
Cedar Gro. *Moi* 3E **24**
Cedar Gro. *Newh* 1H **19**
Cedar Rd. *Cas G* 2F **23**
Celandine Pl. *W'vle* 4B **20**
Central Av. *Ibs* 7B **34**
Central Ct. *Coal* 2E **34**
Central Pas. *Ibs* 7B **34**
Central Rd. *Hug* 3E **34**
Central Way. *Burt T* 7G **9**
Centrum E. Retail Pk. *Burt T* 7D **12**
Centrum 100. *Burt T* 6E **12**
Channing Way. *Elli* 6D **34**
Chapel Clo. *Alb V* 7K **19**
Chapel Clo. *R'stn* 1A **34**
Chapel Clo. *Will* 7J **7**
Chapel La. *A'lw* 2A **12**
Chapel La. *Cole* 1K **27**
Chapel La. *Rol D* 2G **9**
Chapel St. *Cas G* 1F **23**
Chapel St. *Chur G* 7H **19**
Chapel St. *Doni* 1B **30**
Chapel St. *Ibs* 6B **34**
Chapel St. *Mea* 5F **31**
Chapel St. *Newh* 2G **19**
Chapel St. *Oakt* 4C **30**
Chapel St. *Smis* 5J **21**
Chapel St. *W'vle* 6B **20**
Chapmans Mdw. *Ash Z* 5B **26**
Charles St. *Chur G* 6J **19**
Charles St. *Coal* 7B **28**

Charleston Clo. *Newh* 1H 19
Charlotte Ct. *Burt T* 7H 13
Charlton Clo. *L'tn* 4D 22
Charnborough Ct. *Coal* 2J 35
Charnborough Rd. *Coal* 1J 35
Charnwood Rd. *Burt T* 7G 9
Charnwood St. *Coal* 2F 35
Chatfield Clo. *Stape* 6D 14
Chatsworth Dri. *Tut* 7B 4
Chatsworth Rd. *Newh* 2H 19
Chaucer Clo. *Burt T* 1J 13
Cheedale Clo. *Burt T* 2B 14
Cheltenham Dri. *Ash Z* 2K 25
Cherry Ct. *Bran* 7F 13
Cherry Gth. *Hilt* 3J 5
Cherry Leys. *Burt T* 3D 14
Cherry Tree Clo. *Hilt* 3J 5
Cherry Tree Clo. *Newh* 2G 19
Cherry Tree Ct. *Moi* 3E 24
Cherry Tree M. *W'vle* 6C 20
Cherrytree Rd. *Burt T* 2A 18
Chesterfield Av. *Newh* 2F 19
Chesterfield Dri. *L'tn* 3D 22
Chester Gdns. *Chur G* 6J 19
Chesterton Rd. *Burt T* 7J 9
Chestnut Av. *Mid* 2J 19
Chestnut Clo. *Ibs* 7A 34
Chestnut Clo. *Moi* 4E 24
Chestnut Grn. *Chur G* 6J 19
Chestnut Gro. *Coal* 2J 35
Chestnut Gro. *Etw* 1C 6
Chestnut Rd. *Burt T* 1A 18
Chestnut Way. *Rep* 4K 11
Chevin, The. *Stret* 5H 9
Cheviot Clo. *Swad* 5H 19
Chichester Clo. *Elli* 6D 34
Chiltern Ri. *Ash Z* 4B 26
Chiltern Rd. *Swad* 5G 19
Chilton Ct. Stret 5K 9 (off Bridge St.)
Christopher Clo. *Ibs* 5B 34
Chrysanthemum Ct. Newh 3H 19 (off Plummer Rd.)
Church Av. *Hatt* 5C 4
Church Av. *Swad* 5J 19
Chu. Broughton Rd. *Fos* 3B 4
Church Clo. *B'dby* 7E 20
Church Clo. *Burt T* 3C 14
Church Clo. *Will* 1J 11
Chu. Gresley Ind. Est. *Chur G* 1H 23
Church Hill. *Etw* 1C 6
Church Hill. *Swan* 2C 28
Church Hill St. *Burt T* 4C 14
Churchill Clo. *Ash Z* 3J 25
Churchill Dri. *Hilt* 3K 5
Church La. *C'wll* 2A 22
Church La. *Newt S* 6E 10
Church La. *R'stn* 2K 33
Church La. *Swan & Whit* 4C 28
Church M. *Hatt* 4C 4
Church Rd. *Bran* 1D 16
Church Rd. *Egg* 1C 10
Church Rd. *Newh* 2H 19
Church Rd. *Rol D* 1D 8
Church Rd. *Stret* 5K 9
Churchside. *Will* 1H 11
Church St. *Chur G* 7H 19
Church St. *Doni* 2B 30
Church St. *Harts* 2E 20
Church St. *Newh* 2H 19
Church St. *Swad* 4K 19
Church St. *Swep* 7C 32
Church St. *Tut* 6B 4
Church Vw. *Burt T* 7H 9
Church Vw. *Ibs* 7A 34
Church Vw. *Rol D* 2F 9
Church Wlk. Doni 2B 30 (off Church St.)
Church Way. *Over* 7J 23
Churchyard. Ash Z 3B 26 (off Lwr. Church St.)
Churnet Ct. *Burt T* 3K 13
City of Dan. *Whit* 5G 29
City of Three Waters. *Whit* 3F 29
City, The. *W'vle* 6C 20 (in two parts)
Civic Way. *Swad* 4J 19
Clamp Dri. *Swad* 5J 19
Claremont Dri. *R'stn* 7A 28 (in two parts)
Clarence Dri. *Coal* 2G 35
Clarence St. *Burt T* 6H 13
Claridge Pl. *Ash Z* 3A 26
Clarke Clo. *Whit* 5G 29
Clarke Ind. Est. *Burt T* 4K 13
Clarke Rd. *Coal* 2K 35
Claverhouse Rd. *Burt T* 5B 14
Clay Clo. *Swad* 4A 20
Clay La. *Cole* 1B 28
Clay La. *Elli* 7F 35
Claymar Dri. *Newh* 1H 19
Claymills Rd. *Stret* 4A 10
Clay's La. *Bran* 1E 16
Clay St. *Burt T* 6A 14
Clay St. E. *Burt T* 6B 14
Cleave. *Bran* 7F 13
Clematis Cres. *Burt T* 7B 14
Cleveland Clo. *Swad* 5J 19
Clewley Rd. *Bran* 7E 12
Cliffe Hill Rail Terminal. *Elli* 6H 35
Clifton Av. *Ash Z* 1A 26
Clifton Clo. *Over* 6H 23
Clifton Clo. *Swad* 6H 19
Clifton Dri. *Ash Z* 2K 25
Clifton Thorpe Meadows. *Ash Z* 7K 21
Clink La. *Swan* 5B 28
Cloisters, The. *Burt T* 6A 14
Close Bank. *Tut* 7B 4
Close Banks Wlk. *Tut* 7B 4
Close, The. *Alb V* 1A 24
Close, The. *L'tn* 4D 22
Close, The. *Tut* 7A 4
Clover Ct. *Bran* 2D 16
Cloverdale. *Mid* 1J 19
Clover Pl. *Thri* 1E 28
Clover Slade. *Find* 4K 7
Clyde Ct. *Thri* 1E 28
Coach Ho. M. *Newh* 1H 19
Coach Way. *Will* 1K 11
Coalfield Way. *Ash Z* 3D 26
Coalpit La. *Cot E* 7A 22
Coalville Bus. Cen. *Coal* 7E 28
COALVILLE COMMUNITY HOSPITAL. 1H 35
Coalville La. *R'stn* 1A 34
Coleorton La. *Pack* 7B 26
Coleridge Ct. Burt T 1H 13 (off Horninglow Rd.)
College Clo. *Coal* 2D 34
Colliery La. *L'tn* 5E 22
Colliery Rd. *Chur G* 1H 23
Colliery Row. *Chur G* 7H 19
Colliery Trail, Exhibition Hall & Mus. 1C 34
Comet Way. *Coal* 7D 28
Common La. *Tat* 6A 12
Common Rd. *Chur G* 7J 19
Common Side. *Chur G* 6K 19
Coniston Ct. Swad 4J 19 (off Darklands Rd.)
Coniston Gdns. *Ash Z* 4B 26
Convent Clo. *Burt T* 7A 14
Convent Dri. *Coal* 2E 34
Conway Clo. *Stret* 6J 9
Cooper Clo. *Whit* 4E 28
Coopers Cft. *Hatt* 4B 4
Cooper's Sq. *Burt T* 5J 13
Cophills Clo. *Mea* 6F 31
Copperas Rd. *Newh* 3E 18
Coppice Clo. *R'stn* 7A 28
Coppice Side. *Swad* 6K 19
Copse Clo. *Hug* 3D 34
Copse Ri. *Mid* 1J 19
Copson St. *Ibs* 7B 34
Corden Av. *Stret* 6A 10
Corkscrew La. *N Pack & Cole* 5D 26 (in two parts)
Cornmill Balk. *Tut* 7C 4 (in two parts)
Cornmill La. *Tut* 7B 4
Cornwall Rd. *Burt T* 2K 17
Coronation Av. *Moi* 3E 24
Coronation La. *Oakt* 4C 30
Coronation St. *Over* 5H 23
Coronation St. *Swad* 3H 19
Costello Clo. *Ibs* 5B 34
Coton Pk. *L'tn* 6C 18
Coton Rd. *Walt T* 7C 16
Cotswold Clo. *Swad* 5H 19
Cotswold Rd. *Bran* 1E 16
Cotswold Way. *Ash Z* 4B 26
Cottage Clo. *Newh* 2H 19
Cottesmore Clo. *Burt T* 6B 14
Ct. Farm La. *Bran* 1D 16
Courtland Rd. *Etw* 2C 6
Court St. *W'vle* 5B 20
Courtyard, The. *Coal* 7E 28
Coventry Clo. *Mid* 2A 20
Coverdale. *Whit* 3F 29
Covert Pl. *Alb V* 1K 23
Crafty Flats La. *Cot E* 7A 22
Cragdale. *Whit* 2E 28
Craven St. *Burt T* 1H 13
Craythorne Clo. *Newh* 1H 19
Craythorne Golf Cen. 3H 9
Craythorne Rd. *Stret* 3G 9
Crescent Rd. *Hug* 3D 34
Crescent, The. *Newh* 2F 19
Crest Clo. *Stret* 5K 9
Crest, The. *L'tn* 4D 22
Crestwood Clo. *Stret* 6J 9
Creswell Dri. *R'stn* 2K 33
Crichton Av. *Stret* 7J 9
Crich Way. *Newh* 3F 19
Cricket Clo. *Newt S* 6F 11
Cricketers Clo. *Burt T* 7A 14
Croft Clo. *Rol D* 2G 9
Croft, The. *Ash Z* 4C 26
Croft, The. *Burt T* 6A 14
Croft, The. *Coal* 2A 34
Croft, The. *Mea* 5E 30
Croft, The. *Newh* 2F 19
Cromore Clo. *Coal* 1K 35
Cromwell Clo. *Ash Z* 2C 26
Cromwell Clo. *Tut* 1B 8
Cropston Dri. *Coal* 2H 35
Cross La. *Rol D* 4G 9
Crossman St. *Burt T* 4F 13
Cross St. *Burt T* 5H 13
Cross St. *Cas G* 1F 23
Crown Ind. Est. *Burt T* 5G 13
Crusader Clo. *Whit* 4G 29
Culland Rd. *Bran* 1G 17
Cumberland Rd. *Burt T* 1J 17
Cumberland Rd. *Elli* 6E 34
Curlew Clo. *Coal* 2H 35
Curtis Way. *Burt T* 3G 13
Curzon St. *Burt T* 4G 13
Curzon St. *Ibs* 7B 34
Curzon St. W. *Burt T* 4G 13
Cutting, The. *Harts* 4C 20

D

Daisy Clo. *Coal* 2H 35
Daisy Clo. *Doni* 1B 30
Dale Brook. *Hilt* 4K 5
Dalebrook Rd. *Burt T* 2B 14
Dale End La. *Hilt* 2H 5
Dale End Rd. *Hilt* 3H 5
Dalefield Dri. *Swad* 5J 19
Dales Clo. *Newh* 3F 19
Daleside. *Burt T* 6C 14
Dale St. *Burt T* 5H 13
Dalkeith Wlk. *Thri* 1E 28
Dallow Clo. *Burt T* 2H 13
Dallow Cres. *Burt T* 2H 13
Dallow St. *Burt T* 2G 13
Dalston Rd. *Newh* 3H 19
Dalton Av. *Stape* 5C 14
Dame Paulet Wlk. *Burt T* 5J 13
Darklands La. *Swad* 4H 19
Darklands Rd. *Swad* 4J 19
Dark La. *Tat* 6A 12
Darley Clo. *Cas G* 7H 19
Darley Clo. *Stape* 6D 14
Darley Dale. *Chur G* 6G 19
Darwin Clo. *Stape* 6D 14
Davis Rd. *Swad* 4J 19
Dawkins Rd. *Doni* 1B 30
Daybell Rd. *Moi* 5D 24

Dayton Clo. *Coal* 7B **28**
Deepdale Clo. *Burt T* 2C **14**
Deepdale Clo. *Ibs* 6B **34**
De Ferrers Cft. *Stret* 6H **9**
Degens Way. *Hug* 3C **34**
Delhi Clo. *Burt T* 4D **14**
Denbigh Clo. *Stret* 7J **9**
Denby Turn. *Burt T* 2J **13**
Dennis St. *Hug* 4E **34**
Denstone Clo. *Ash Z* 1K **25**
Denton Ri. *Burt T* 7F **9**
Denton Rd. *Burt T* 1F **13**
Derby Rd. *Ash Z* 2A **26**
Derby Rd. *Burt T & Stret* 2J **13**
Derby Rd. *Hatt* 3C **4**
Derby Rd. *Hilt & Etw* 3J **5**
Derby Rd. *Swad* 4K **19**
Derby Rd. *Tickn & Smis* 1H **21**
Derby Southern By-Pass. *Hilt & Etw* 2A **6**
Derby St. *Burt T* 4H **13**
Derby St. E. *Burt T* 3H **13**
Derry's Hollow. *Elli* 7F **35**
De Ruthyn Clo. *Moi* 5D **24**
Derwent Clo. *Burt T* 4K **13**
Derwent Clo. *Cas G* 7H **19**
Derwent Ct. *Will* 7H **7**
Derwent Gdns. *Ash Z* 5B **26**
Derwent Pk. *Burt T* 2K **13**
Derwent Rd. *Burt T* 6B **14**
Devana Av. *Coal* 2G **35**
Deveron Clo. *Coal* 1K **35**
Deveron Clo. *Stret* 5H **9**
Devon Clo. *Burt T* 2K **17**
Devon Clo. *Moi* 3F **25**
Dibble Rd. *Bran* 1F **17**
Dickens Clo. *Burt T* 1J **13**
Dickens Dri. *Swad* 3K **19**
Dingle, The. *Burt T* 7K **13**
Dinmore Grange. *Harts* 2E **20**
Discovery Golf & Leisure. 2B 34
(Pitch & Putt Course)
Discovery Way. *Ash Z* 2C **26**
Dish La. *Hilt* 1G **5**
Dodslow Av. *Rol D* 3G **9**
Doles La. *Find* 2K **7**
Dominion Rd. *Swad* 3J **19**
Donington Dri. *Ash Z* 4K **25**
Donington le Heath Manor House. 4D 34
Donisthorpe La. *Moi* 6A **24**
Donithorne Clo. *Burt T* 7H **9**
Dorset Clo. *Burt T* 2K **17**
Dorset Dri. *Moi* 3F **25**
Douglas Dri. *Ibs* 7B **34**
Dovecliff Cres. *Stret* 4A **10**
Dovecliff Rd. *Rol D & Stret* 2K **9**
Dove Clo. *W'vle* 5C **20**
Dovedale Clo. *Burt T* 3B **14**
Dove Gro. *Egg* 1B **10**
Dove Lea. *Rol D* 2G **9**
Dover Ct. *Burt T* 7H **9**
Doveridge Rd. *Burt T* 5C **14**
Dove Ri. *Hilt* 3H **5**
Dove Rd. *Coal* 3H **35**
Dover Rd. *Burt T* 7G **9**
Dove Side. *Hatt* 5C **4**
Dove Vw. *Tut* 7B **4**
Downside Dri. *Ash Z* 2K **25**
Drayton St. *Swad* 4K **19**
Drift Clo. *B'dby* 1E **24**
Drift Side. *B'dby* 2E **24**
Drive, The. *Burt T* 7H **9**
Drome Clo. *Coal* 1K **35**
Dryden Clo. *Mea* 6F **31**
Duchy Clo. *Stret* 6K **9**
Duck St. *Egg* 1B **10**
Duke St. *Burt T* 5H **13**
Duke St. *Tut* 7B **4**
Dumps Rd. *Whit* 3F **29**
Dunbar Rd. *Coal* 2K **35**
Dunbar Way. *Ash Z* 3B **26**
Dundee Rd. *Mid* 3A **20**
Dunedin Cres. *Burt T* 5D **14**
Dunnsmoor La. *Harts* 1A **20**
Dunsmore Way. *Mid* 3A **20**
Dunstall Brook. *Burt T* 6B **14**
Durban Clo. *Burt T* 4D **14**
Durham Clo. *Mid* 3B **20**
Durris Clo. *Coal* 1K **35**
Dyson's Clo. *Mea* 6E **30**

E

Eagle Clo. *Mea* 6E **30**
Eagle Heights. *Burt T* 4E **14**
Earls Ct. *Stret* 6J **9**
East Cres. *Elli* 7F **35**
E. End Dri. *Swad* 4K **19**
Eastern Av. *Burt T* 6A **10**
Eastfield Rd. *Mid* 2K **19**
East Lawn. *Find* 3K **7**
East St. *Burt T* 4C **14**
East Wlk. *Ibs* 7B **34**
Eaton Clo. *Hatt* 4C **4**
Edgecote Dri. *Newh* 1H **19**
Edinburgh Way. *Stret* 6J **9**
Edmonton Pl. *Burt T* 4E **14**
Edward St. *Alb V* 7K **19**
Edward St. *Burt T* 3G **13**
Edward St. *Harts* 5D **20**
Edward St. *Over* 5J **23**
Egginton Rd. *Etw* 4C **6**
Egginton Rd. *Hilt* 3J **5**
Eighth Av. *Burt T* 7E **12**
Eldon St. *Burt T* 4C **14**
Electric St. *Burt T* 2K **13**
Electric St. Ind. Est. *Burt T* 2K **13**
Elford St. *Ash Z* 3A **26**
Elgin Wlk. *Thri* 1E **28**
Elizabeth Av. *Ibs* 6B **34**
Elizabeth Av. *Rol D* 3G **9**
Elm Av. *Ash Z* 2C **26**
Elm Clo. *Bran* 7E **12**
Elm Clo. *Ibs* 7A **34**
Elm Dri. *Hilt* 3J **5**
Elm Gro. *Moi* 3E **24**
Elmhurst. *Egg* 1B **10**
Elmsdale Rd. *Harts* 5D **20**
Elms Gro. *Etw* 2D **6**
Elmsleigh Clo. *Mid* 2J **19**
Elmsleigh Dri. *Mid* 2J **19**
Elmsleigh Grn. *Mid* 2J **19**
Elms Rd. *Burt T* 5A **14**
Elsdon Clo. *Whit* 4E **28**
Elstead La. *B'dby* 7E **20**
Elvaston Ct. *Ash Z* 4B **26**
Elwyn Clo. *Stret* 5J **9**
Ely Clo. *Mid* 2A **20**
Emery Clo. *L'tn* 4E **22**
Empire Rd. *Burt T* 4E **14**
Enderby Ri. *Burt T* 7F **9**
End, The. *Newt S* 6F **11**
Enfield Clo. *Hilt* 3K **5**
Ennerdale Gdns. *Ash Z* 4C **26**
Epsom Clo. *Bran* 1E **16**
Ernest Hall Way. *Swad* 4K **19**
Escolme Clo. *Swad* 4A **20**
Essex Rd. *Burt T* 2J **17**
Eton Clo. *Ash Z* 1K **25**
Eton Clo. *Burt T* 1K **13**
Eton Pk. *Burt T* 1K **13**
Eton Rd. *Burt T* 1J **13**
Etta's Way. *Etw* 1C **6**
Etwall By-Pass. *Etw* 1B **6**
Etwall Leisure Cen. 1C 6
Etwall Rd. *Egg* 5H **7**
Etwall Rd. *Etw* 5C **6**
Eureka Rd. *Mid* 3K **19**
Evergreens, The. *Stret* 6A **10**
Evershed Way. *Burt T* 5H **13**
Exeter Clo. *Mid* 2B **20**
Exmoor Clo. *Elli* 6E **34**
Eyam Clo. *Burt T* 5C **14**
Eyrie, The. *Burt T* 4D **14**

F

Fabis Clo. *Swad* 5H **19**
Fairfax Clo. *Ash Z* 2C **26**
Fairfield. *Ibs* 7B **34**
Fairfield Av. *Rol D* 2J **9**
Fairfield Ct. *Hug* 4D **34**
Fairfield Cres. *Newh* 3F **19**
Fairfield Rd. *Hug* 4D **34**
Fairfield Ter. *W'vle* 5C **20**
Fairham Rd. *Stret* 5A **10**
Fairway. *Bran* 2G **17**
Fairway, The. *Newh* 3F **19**
Falaise Way. *Hilt* 3K **5**
Falcon Clo. *Burt T* 2K **13**
Falcon Way. *W'vle* 5C **20**
Faldo Clo. *Bran* 2G **17**
Faraday Av. *Stret* 6J **9**
Farm Clo. *Burt T* 7G **9**
Farm Ct. Flats. Burt T 7H **9**
(off Farm Rd.)
Farm La. *Don H* 4C **34**
Farm La. *Newt S* 7E **10**
Farm Rd. *Burt T* 7H **9**
Farm Side. *Newh* 3G **19**
Farm Town La. *Cole* 3G **27**
Farndale. *Whit* 3E **28**
Fauld La. *Tut* 7A **4**
Faversham Rd. *Burt T* 1F **13**
Featherbed La. *Ash Z* 2C **26**
Femwork Ind. Est. *Burt T* 2K **13**
Fenton Av. *B'dby* 7E **20**
Fenton Clo. *Mea* 7E **30**
Fenton Cres. *Mea* 7F **31**
Fern Av. *Will* 7K **7**
Fern Clo. *Will* 7K **7**
Ferndale. *Ibs* 7A **34**
Ferrers Av. *Tut* 1A **8**
Ferrers Clo. *Ash Z* 4J **25**
Ferrers Rd. *Whit* 5G **29**
Ferry Grn. *Will* 1J **11**
Ferry St. *Burt T* 1K **17**
Ferry Va. Clo. *Burt T* 7K **13**
Festival Rd. *Bran* 1D **16**
Fettes Clo. *Ash Z* 1K **25**
Fiddler's La. *Tut* 3D **8**
Field Av. *Hatt* 4B **4**
Field Clo. *Burt T* 7F **9**
Field Clo. *Hilt* 3J **5**
Field Clo. *Thri* 2E **28**
Field Dri. *Rol D* 2G **9**
Field La. *B'dry* 6F **21**
Field La. *Burt T* 7D **8**
Field Ri. *Burt T* 7F **9**
Fields La. *Cas G* 3G **23**
Field Way. Newh 3G **19**
(off South Dri.)
Fifth Av. *Burt T* 5F **13**
Finch Clo. *W'vle* 5C **20**
Findern La. *Burna* 1H **7**
Findern La. *Will* 7H **7**
Finney Clo. *Doni* 1B **30**
First Av. *Burt T* 7D **12**
Fir Tree Wlk. Moi 3E **24**
(off Ashfield Dri.)
Fisher Clo. *Rep* 4K **11**
Fishing Ponds & Nature Trail. 2B 34
Fishpond La. *Egg* 1B **10**
Fishpond La. *Tut* 7A **4**
Five Lands Rd. *Burt T* 7A **14**
Flagstaff 42 Bus. Pk. *Ash Z* 2C **26**
Flatts Clo. *Burt T* 1G **13**
Flax Cft. *Hatt* 4B **4**
Fleet St. *Burt T* 5J **13**
Fletches, The. *Stret* 5G **9**
Floret Clo. *R'stn* 7B **28**
Foan Hill. *Swan* 5C **28**
Fontwell Rd. *Bran* 1E **16**
Fordice Clo. *Hug* 3D **34**
Ford La. *Will* 1J **11**
Ford St. *Burt T* 1K **17**
Forest Rd. *Burt T* 2C **12**
Forest Rd. *Hug & Coal* 3E **34**
Forge Clo. *Rep* 4K **11**
Forge La. *Stret* 4A **10**
Forman Clo. *Swad* 4J **19**
Formans Way. *R'stn* 7B **28**
Forrester Clo. *Cole* 5J **27**
Forties La. *Smis* 4J **21**
Fosbrooke Clo. *R'stn* 2K **33**
Foster Rd. *W'vle* 6C **20**
Foston Av. *Burt T* 1F **13**
Foston Clo. *Hatt* 5B **4**
Foston/Hatton/Hilton By-Pass.
Hatt & Fos 1A **4**

Fourth Av. *Burt T* 5E **12**
Fox Clo. *Bran* 7G **13**
Foxglove Av. *Burt T* 7B **14**
Foxglove Rd. *Coal* 2H **35**
Franklin Clo. *Stape* 6C **14**
Franks Rd. *Bar H* 6K **35**
Frearson Rd. *Hug* 3C **34**
Frederick St. *Burt T* 7K **13**
Frederick St. *W'vle* 5B **20**
Friars Wlk. *Burt T* 5K **13**
Friary Cft. *Newh* 1H **19**
Fulton Dri. *Coal* 7B **28**
Furnace La. *Moi* 6B **24**
Furnace La. Ind. Est. *Moi* 6B **24**
Fyfield Rd. *Burt T* 2K **17**

G

Gables, The. *Ash Z* 5B **26**
Gables, The. *Newh* 3F **19**
Gainsborough Way. *Burt T* 4C **14**
Galahad Dri. *Stret* 4K **9**
Gallows La. *Mea* 7H **31**
Gamble Clo. *Ibs* 5B **34**
Garden Rd. *Coal* 7F **29**
Garendon Rd. *Coal* 2J **35**
Garfield Rd. *Hug* 3D **34**
Garganey Clo. *Coal* 2H **35**
Gartan Rd. *Bran* 7F **13**
Gatcombe Clo. *Stret* 5J **9**
Gawain Gro. *Stret* 4K **9**
Geary Clo. *Whit* 4E **28**
Geary La. *Bret* 6G **15**
Gelsmoor Rd. *Cole* 1A **28**
Genista Clo. *Burt T* 7B **14**
George Holmes Bus. Pk. *Swad* 5G **19**
George Holmes Way. *Swad* 4G **19**
George St. *Burt T* 4J **13**
George St. *Chur G* 6H **19**
George St. *Whit* 5G **29**
George Walker Ct. *Burt T* 2H **13**
Georgian Crystal. *7B 4* *(off Silk Mill La.)*
Gerard Gro. *Etw* 1D **6**
Gillamore Dri. *Whit* 7H **29**
Gladstone St. *Ibs* 7B **34**
Glamis Clo. *Stret* 6J **9**
Glebe Clo. *Rol D* 2F **9**
Glebe Rd. *Thri* 1D **28**
Glebe St. *Swad* 5J **19**
Glebe Vw. *Coal* 7A **28**
Glenalmond Clo. *Ash Z* 2K **25**
Glen Av. *Ibs* 7C **34**
Glencroft Clo. *Burt T* 1G **17**
Gleneagles Dri. *Stret* 5H **9**
Glenfield Ri. *Burt T* 7F **9**
Glen Ri. *Burt T* 7F **9**
Glensyl Way. *Burt T* 3K **13**
Glen Way. *Coal* 3G **35**
Gloucester Way. *Burt T* 6C **14**
Goliath Rd. *Coal* 7E **28**
Goodman St. *Burt T* 2J **13**
Goodwood Clo. *Stret* 5H **9**
Gordon St. *Burt T* 3H **13**
Gorse La. *Moi* 3B **24**
Gorse Rd. *Hug* 4D **34**
Gorsey Leys. *Over* 6K **23**
Gorsty Leys. *Find* 4K **7**
Goseley Av. *Harts* 4D **20**
Goseley Cres. *Harts* 4D **20**
Gough Side. *Burt T* 5J **13**
Gracedieu. *Whit* 1G **29**
Gracedieu Rd. *Whit* 2E **28**
Grafton Rd. *Burt T* 6B **14**
Graham Clo. *Bran* 1H **17**
Grain Warehouse Yd. *Burt T* 4H **13**
Grange Clo. *Ash Z* 4K **25**
Grange Clo. *Burt T* 3G **13** (in two parts)
Grange Ct. *Egg* 1C **10**
Grange Rd. *Hug* 4E **34**
Grange Rd. *Ibs* 7B **34**
Grange Rd. *Newh* 3F **19**
Grange St. *Burt T* 4G **13**
Grange, The. *Burt T* 4G **13**
Grange, The. *Pack* 7B **26**
Granville Clo. *Hatt* 4C **4**
Granville Ct. Swad 4K 19 *(off Hall Farm Rd.)*
Granville Ind. Est. *Chur G* 6A **20**
Granville M. *W'vle* 5B **20**
Granville St. *W'vle* 5B **20**
Grasmere. *Coal* 7J **29**
Grasmere Clo. *Burt T* 6C **14**
Grassy La. *Mea* 4G **31**
Greenacres. *Coal* 1J **35**
Greenbank Leisure Cen. **4J** 19
Green Clo. *Will* 7H **7**
Greenfield Dri. *L'tn* 3D **22**
Greenfield Rd. *Mea* 5G **31**
Greenfields Dri. *Coal* 1H **35**
Greenhill Rd. *Coal* 1H **35**
Green Lands. *Mid* 1J **19**
Green La. *Burna* 1G **7**
Green La. *Burt T* 7G **9**
Green La. *Over* 5G **23** (in two parts)
Green La. *Tut* 1B **8** (in two parts)
Green La. *Whit* 6F **29**
Greenline Bus. Pk. *Burt T* 4G **13**
Greenside Clo. *Doni* 1B **30**
Green St. *Burt T* 6J **13**
Green, The. *Ash Z* 3A **26**
Green, The. *Bret* 4H **15**
Green, The. *Don H* 5D **34**
Green, The. *Stret* 5K **9**
Green, The. *Thri* 2E **28**
Green, The. *Will* 7H **7** (in two parts)
Greenvale Clo. *Burt T* 7A **14**
Greenway. *Burt T* 3B **14**
Greenwood Rd. *Burt T* 7K **13**
Gregson Clo. *Swad* 3J **19**
Gresley Rovers F.C. **7J** 19
Gresley Woodlands. *Chur G* 6H **19**
Gresley Wood Rd. *Swad & Chur G* 5G **19**
Gretton Av. *Stret* 5K **9**
Griffith Gdns. *Ash Z* 4J **25**
Grizedale Clo. *Burt T* 6C **14**
Grove Pk. *Etw* 3C **6**
Grove Rd. *Whit* 5F **29**
Grove St. *Swad* 4J **19**
Grove, The. *Tat* 7A **12**
Grunmore Dri. *Stret* 4K **9**
Guildford Av. *Mid* 2B **20**
Guild St. *Burt T* 4J **13**
Guinevere Av. *Stret* 4K **9**
Gunby Hill. *N'seal* 7G **23**
Gutteridge St. *Coal* 1D **34**

H

Hackett Clo. *Ash Z* 3A **26**
Hailebury Av. *Ash Z* 2K **25**
Halcyon Ct. *Burt T* 3G **13**
Halcyon Way. *Burt T* 3G **13**
Halifax Clo. *Hilt* 3K **5**
Hallams Row. *Burt T* 3H **13**
Hall Clo. *B'dby* 1F **25**
Hallcroft Av. *Over* 6J **23**
Hall Farm Clo. *Swad* 4K **19**
Hall Farm Rd. *Swad* 4K **19**
Hallfields Rd. *Stant* 4D **18** (in two parts)
Hall Gdns. *R'stn* 2J **33**
Hall Gate. *Coal* 2K **35**
Hall Green Av. *Stret* 4K **9**
Hall Grounds. *Rol D* 2F **9**
Hall La. *Doni* 2B **30**
Hall La. *Pack* 7A **26**
Hall La. *Whit* 5G **29**
Hall La. *Will* 1J **11**
Hall Rd. *Rol D* 2E **8**
Hall St. *Chur G* 6H **19**
Hall St. *Ibs* 7A **34**
Hamilton Dri. *Swad* 3K **19**
Hamilton Fields. *Burt T* 5B **14**
Hamilton Gro. *Swad* 3A **20**
Hamilton Rd. *Burt T* 5B **14**
Hamilton Rd. *Coal* 2K **35**
Hamilton Ter. *Will* 1J **11**
Hanbury Av. *Hatt* 4C **4**
Hanbury Rd. *A'lw* 1A **12**
Hanchurch Clo. *Burt T* 3B **14**
Handsacre Clo. *Swad* 5G **19**
Harbin Rd. *Walt T* 7C **16**
Harbury St. *Burt T* 1F **13**
Harcourt Rd. *Bran* 7D **12**
Harebell Clo. *W'vle* 4B **20**
Harehedge La. *Burt T* 6G **9**
Hargate Rd. *Stape* 6D **14**
Harlaxton St. *Burt T* 1F **13**
Harlech Way. *Stret* 6J **9**
Harper Av. *Burt T* 7H **9**
Harper Ct. *Burt T* 7H **9**
Harratts Clo. *Ibs* 7B **34**
Harrison Clo. *Bran* 7G **13**
Harrow Clo. *Ash Z* 1K **25**
Harrow Dri. *Burt T* 7H **13**
Harrow Rd. *Mid* 1J **19**
Hartshill Rd. *Harts* 4D **20**
Hartshorne Rd. *W'vle* 5C **20**
Harvest Gro. *Moi* 4D **24**
Harvest Hill. *Mid* 1J **19**
Harvey Rd. *Bran* 7F **13**
Harwood Av. *Bran* 7D **12**
Haslyn Wlk. *Coal* 2J **35** (in two parts)
Hassall Rd. *Hatt* 4C **4**
Hastings Av. *Whit* 5H **29**
Hastings Rd. *Swad* 5J **19**
Hastings, The. *Ibs* 6B **34**
Hastings Way. *Ash Z* 4B **26**
Hawfield La. *Burt T* 4C **14** (Chu. Hill St., in two parts)
Hawfield La. *Burt T* 3E **14** (Sales La.)
Hawkins La. *Burt T* 3J **13**
Hawkins La. Ind. Est. Burt T 2K 13 *(off Hawkins La.)*
Hawk's Dri. *Burt T* 4E **14**
Hawksley Dri. *Rol D* 2G **9**
Hawley Clo. *Hug* 4F **35**
Hawthorn Clo. *Coal* 1F **35**
Hawthorn Clo. *Hilt* 4J **5**
Hawthorn Cres. *Burt T* 1A **18**
Hawthorn Cres. *Find* 3K **7**
Hawthorne Clo. *Mea* 4F **31**
Hawthorn Ri. *Newh* 1G **19**
Haydock Clo. *Bran* 1F **17**
Hayes Clo. *Whit* 5G **29**
Hayes, The. *Find* 4K **7**
Hayes, The. *Hatt* 3B **4**
Hay Wain La. *Mid* 1J **19**
Hay Wlk. *Burt T* 5K **13**
Hazel Clo. *Mea* 5F **31**
Hazel Clo. *Newh* 3H **19**
Hazel Gro. *Moi* 3E **24**
Hazelwood Rd. *Burt T* 2K **17**
HCM Ind. Est. *Burt T* 3K **13**
Headingley Clo. *Coal* 3H **35**
Hearthcote Rd. *Swad* 6G **19**
Hearthcote Rd. Ind. Est. *Swad* 4H **19**
Heart of the National Forest Vis. Cen. **5A** 24
Heatherdale. *Ibs* 7A **34**
Heather Ho. *Heat* 7G **33**
Heather La. *Norm H* 4E **32**
Heather La. *Pack* 1B **32**
Heather La. *R'stn* 5H **33**
Heather St John Sports & Social Club. **7G** 33
Heathfield. *Thri* 1F **29**
Heath La. *B'dry & Smis* 7F **21** (in two parts)
Heath La. *Find* 5K **7** (in two parts)
Heath Rd. *Burt T* 1K **17**
Heath Way. *Hatt* 5B **4**
Hector Rd. *Coal* 7E **28**
Hedge Gro. *Mid* 1J **19**
Hedge Rd. *Hug* 3D **34**
Helmsdale Clo. *Coal* 1K **35**
Helston Clo. *L'tn* 4E **22**
Henhurst Hill. *Burt T* 3A **12**
Henhurst Ridge. *Burt T* 3B **12**
Henshurst Farm. *Burt T* 2C **12**
Henson's La. *Thri* 1E **28**

Herbert St. Burt T 4C 14
Hereford Cres. Mid 2A 20
Heritage Way. Burt T 6B 14
Hermitage Ct. Whit 6F 29
Hermitage Ind. Est., The. Coal 7E 28
Hermitage Leisure Cen. 5F 29
Hermitage Pk. Way. Newh 1H 19
Hermitage Rd. Whit 6E 28
Heron Dri. W'vle 5C 20
Heron Way. Coal 2G 35
Hervey Woods. Whit 4F 29
Higgins Rd. Newh 2G 19
Higgott Clo. Bran 7F 13
High Bank Rd. Burt T 4C 14
Highcroft Dri. Burt T 3E 12
High Cross. Cas G 1F 23
Highfield Clo. Burt T 7F 9
Highfield Dri. Burt T 4A 14
Highfield Rd. Swad 5J 19
Highfields Clo. Ash Z 3J 25
Highfields Clo. L'tn 3D 22
Highfield St. Coal 3C 34
Highfield St. Swad 5J 19
Highgate. Ash Z 1K 25
Highgrove Clo. Stret 5J 9
Highlands Dri. Burt T 3B 14
High St. Burt T 5J 13
High St. Coal 1D 34
High St. Ibs 7B 34
High St. L'tn 4C 22
High St. Mea 6F 31
High St. Newh 2G 19
High St. Pack 7B 26
High St. Rep 4K 11
High St. Swad 4K 19
High St. Tut 7B 4
High St. W'vle 5C 20
Hilary Cres. Whit 6H 29
Hillcrest. Tut 1A 8
Hillcrest Av. Burt T 3B 14
Hillfield La. Stret 5K 9
Hill Ri. Mea 4F 31
Hillsdale Rd. Burt T 2C 14
Hillside. Find 4K 7
Hillside. Tut 7A 4
Hillside Gdns. Chur G 6G 19
Hillside Rd. L'tn 3D 22
Hill St. Ash Z 3K 25
Hill St. Burt T 1K 17
Hill St. Doni 1B 30
Hill St. Newh 2G 19
Hill St. Swad 5K 19
Hilltop Ind. Est. Bar H 6K 35
Hilton Clo. Newh 1H 19
Hilton Depot. Hilt 5K 5
Hilton Rd. Egg 6B 6
Hilton Rd. Etw 1B 6
Hobart Clo. Burt T 5D 14
Hockley, The. Whit 4G 29
Hogarth Rd. Whit 4G 29
Holcombe Clo. Whit 3F 29
Holdings, The. Chur G 7H 19
Holland Clo. Whit 4F 29
Hollies Clo. Newt S 6F 11
Hollow Cres. Burt T 3D 14
Hollow La. Burt T 3D 14
Hollow, The. Norm H 4E 32
Holly Bank. Hug 4E 34
Holly Bank Clo. Newh 1H 19
Holly Clo. Moi 3E 24
Holly Ct. W'vle 6C 20
Holly Grn. Burt T 7A 14
Holly Hayes Rd. Whit 5G 29
Hollyhock Way. Bran 1D 16
Holly Rd. Mea 5F 31
Holly St. Burt T 7A 14
Holme Clo. Hatt 4B 4
Holme Farm Av. Burt T 7A 14
Holmes Ct. Hug 4E 34
Holts La. Don H 4C 34
Holt's La. Tut 1A 8
Holyoake Cres. Heat 7H 33
Holyoake Dri. Heat 7H 33
Holywell Av. Ash Z 2A 26
Home Cft. Dri. Pack 7A 26
Home Farm Cvn. Site. Rol D 2F 9
Home Farm Ct. Cas G 7E 18
Homestead Rd. Thri 1E 28
Honeysuckle Clo. Coal 2H 35
Honeysuckle Clo. Newh 2H 19
Honeysuckle Vw. Burt T 7B 14
Hood Ct. Ash Z 3A 26
(off North St.)
Hood Pk. Leisure Cen. 2A 26
Hoon La. Hilt 2F 5
Hoon Ridge. Hilt 1F 5
Hoon Rd. Hatt 5C 4
Hopley Rd. A'lw 2A 12
Hopmeadow Way. Burt T 6B 14
Hornbrook Clo. Burt T 6G 9
Hornbrook Rd. Burt T 7G 9
Horninglow Rd. Burt T 1H 13
Horninglow Rd. N. Burt T 7G 9
Horninglow St. Burt T 3J 13
Hornton Rd. Burt T 7G 9
Horses La. Mea 6G 31
Horton Av. Stret 7A 10
Hospital La. R'stn 2K 33
Hospital La. Swan 2C 28
Hotel St. Coal 1E 34
Hough Hill. Swan 6B 28
Howden Clo. Newh 3H 19
Howe Ct. Whit 4E 28
Howe Rd. Whit 4E 28
Hunter St. Burt T 2H 13
Huntingdon Ct. Ash Z 3A 26
Huntingdon Rd. Ash Z 4J 25
Huntingdon Rd. Burt T 1J 17
Huntingdon Way. Mea 5D 30
Huntspill Rd. Hilt 4K 5
Hurst Dri. Stret 5K 9
Hylton Clo. Burt T 1F 17

I

Ibstock Ind. Est. Ibs 6C 34
Ibstock Rd. Elli 7D 34
Ibstock Rd. R'stn 2A 34
Ibstock St. Burt T 1G 13
Imex Bus. Pk. Burt T 4G 13
Ingleby Clo. Swad 5G 19
Ingle Dri. Ash Z 2J 25
Interlink Ind. Pk. Elli 7J 35
Ironwalls La. Tut 1B 8
Ivanhoe Dri. Ash Z 3J 25
Ivanhoe Ind. Est. Ash Z 1K 25
(in two parts)
Ivanhoe Way. Ash Z 2B 26
Ivanhoe Way. Moi 6C 24
(Measham Rd.)
Ivanhoe Way. Moi 7B 24
(Poplar Av.)
Iveagh Clo. Mea 5G 31
Ivy Clo. Doni 1B 30
Ivy Clo. Will 1H 11
Ivy Ct. Etw 1C 6
Ivy Ct. Hilt 4J 5
Ivy Gro. Burt T 7H 9
Ivy Lodge Clo. Burt T 1K 17

J

Jacklin Clo. Bran 2F 17
Jackson Av. Stret 7A 10
Jacksons La. Etw 3C 6
Jackson St. Coal 1D 34
Jacks Wlk. Hug 3C 34
Jacobean Ct. Burt T 3D 14
Jacques St. Ibs 6B 34
James Brindley Way. Stret 5A 10
James Ct. Burt T 5J 13
(off James St.)
James St. Burt T 5H 13
James St. Coal 2D 34
James St. Mid 3A 20
Jarvis Way. Whit 4F 29
Jasmine Clo. Burt T 7B 14
Jeffcoats La. Swan 3C 28
Jennings Way. Burt T 4F 13
Jenny's La. R'stn 2A 34
Jephson Clo. Burt T 1G 17
Jerram's La. Burt T 7K 13
Jewsbury Av. Mea 5G 31
Jinny Clo. Hatt 5B 4
Jinny Nature Trail. 2J 9
John Port Clo. Etw 1D 6
John St. Chur G 6K 19
John St. Newh 2F 19
John St. Swad 3K 19
John St. Thri 2E 28
Jordan Av. Stret 4A 10
Jubilee Ter. Doni 1B 30

K

Kane Clo. Coal 1C 34
Kay Dri. Newh 3G 19
Keats Dri. Swad 2K 19
Keble Clo. Burt T 5D 14
Kedleston Clo. Stret 5H 9
Kelso Clo. Ash Z 3B 26
Kelso Clo. Mea 4F 31
Kelso Ct. Thri 1F 29
Kempton Rd. Burt T 4B 14
Kendal Pl. Elli 6E 34
Kendal Rd. Elli 6E 34
Kendricks Clo. Harts 1D 20
Kenilworth Av. Stret 7J 9
Kenilworth Dri. Ash Z 4B 26
Kenmore Cres. Coal 1K 35
Kensington Rd. Burt T 4B 14
Kent Rd. Burt T 2K 17
Kestrel Av. W'vle 5C 20
Kestrel Way. Burt T 4D 14
Kilburn Way. Newh 3G 19
Kiln Cft. Etw 1D 6
Kiln Way. W'vle 5A 20
Kilwardby St. Ash Z 3K 25
Kimberley Dri. Burt T 4D 14
Kinder Av. Newh 3H 19
King Edward Pl. Burt T 4G 13
Kingfisher Av. W'vle 5C 20
Kingfisher Clo. Whit 7J 29
King George Av. Ash Z 2K 25
King John's Rd. Whit 3G 29
King Richard's Hill. Whit 4G 29
Kingsbury Clo. Burt T 3B 14
Kingsdale Cft. Stret 6J 9
Kingsley Rd. Burt T 7J 9
Kings Rd. Swad 3J 19
Kingston Rd. Burt T 5D 14
King St. Burt T 7H 13
King St. Coal 2E 34
Kingsway. Bran 7G 13
Kinver Rd. Burt T 3B 14
Kirkhill Clo. Coal 1K 35
Kirton Rd. Coal 1K 35
Kitling Greaves La. Burt T 6F 9
Knightsbridge Way. Stret 7J 9
Knights Clo. Ash Z 2K 25
Knights Ct. Stret 5K 9
Knight's Gth. Whit 4G 29
Knight's La. Bret 4H 15
Knob Fields. Cas G 1F 23
Knoll, The. Mid 2J 19
Knowles Hill. Rol D 3G 9
Koppe Clo. Moi 3E 24

L

Laburnum Rd. Burt T 2A 18
Laburnum Rd. Newh 2H 19
Laburnum Way. Etw 2D 6
Ladle End La. Walt T 7C 16
Ladybower Clo. Swad 5H 19
Ladyfields. Mid 2A 20
Ladywell Clo. Stret 5K 9
Lagoona Pk. Over 6K 23
Lakeside Vw. Whit 6F 29
Lancaster Clo. Coal 1K 35
Lancaster Dri. Hilt 3K 5
Lancaster Dri. Tut 1A 8
Lancelot Dri. Stret 5K 9
Langer Clo. Bran 2F 17
Langton Clo. Whit 3F 29
Lansdowne Rd. Bran 1E 16
Lansdowne Rd. Swad 5H 19

Lansdowne Ter. *Burt T* 2J **13**
Larch Rd. *Newh* 1G **19**
Latham Clo. *Burt T* 5D **14**
Lathkill Dale. *Chur G* 6G **19**
Laud Clo. *Ibs* 7A **34**
Launceston Dri. *Hug* 3D **34**
Laurel Gro. *Burt T* 3K **17**
Lawn Av. *Etw* 1D **6**
Lawns Dri. *Newh* 1H **19**
Lawns, The. *Rol D* 2F **9**
Lawrence Clo. *Elli* 6D **34**
Leamington Rd. *Bran* 1D **16**
Leander Ri. *Burt T* 7A **14**
Leawood Rd. *Mid* 1A **20**
Leedhams Cft. *Walt T* 7C **16**
Lees Cres. *Whit* 4H **29**
Legion Dri. *Ibs* 7B **34**
Leicester Rd. *Ash Z & N Pack* 3B **26**
Leicester Rd. *Cole* 6H **27**
Leicester Rd. *Ibs* 6B **34**
Leicester Rd. *Mea* 5G **31**
Leicester Rd. *R'stn* 2K **33**
Leicester Rd. *Whit* 5G **29**
Leicester St. *Burt T* 7H **13**
Leith Clo. *Ash Z* 4C **26**
Lewis Dri. *Burt T* 7G **9**
Leyburn Clo. *Chur G* 7J **19**
Ley Cft. *Hatt* 4B **4**
Leyfields Farm M. *A'lw* 1B **12**
Leys, The. *Newh* 3F **19**
Lichfield Av. *Mid* 3B **20**
Lichfield Rd. *Bar N & Bran* 7A **16**
Lichfield St. *Burt T* 6J **13**
Lilac Gro. *Burt T* 2A **18**
Lily Bank. *Thri* 1D **28**
Limby Hall La. *Swan* 3A **28**
Lime Av. *Mea* 4F **31**
Lime Ct. *Stape* 1K **17**
Lime Gro. *Burt T* 2K **17**
Lime Gro. *Hatt* 3C **4**
Limes, The. *R'stn* 7B **28**
Limestone Clo. *Harts* 5C **20**
Lime Tree Av. *Mid* 1J **19**
Lincoln Rd. *Burt T* 1J **17**
Lincoln Way. *Mid* 3B **20**
Linden Clo. *Ibs* 6A **34**
Linden Way. *Coal* 7D **28**
Linford Cres. *Coal* 1J **35**
Lingfield Rd. *Bran* 1E **16**
Links Clo. *Hug* 4E **34**
Linton Heath. *L'tn* 4F **23**
Linton Rd. *Cas G* 2F **23**
Lit. Burton E. *Burt T* 2J **13**
Lit. Burton W. *Burt T* 3J **13**
Little Clo. *Swad* 3J **19**
Little La. *Pack* 7A **26**
Lit. Thorn Ind. Est. *W'vle* 7C **20**
Locksley Clo. *Ash Z* 2K **25**
Lockton Clo. *Ash Z* 2B **26**
Lodge Clo. *Ash Z* 4K **25**
Lodge Clo. *Etw* 1D **6**
Lodge Hill. *Tut* 3D **8**
Lohengrin Ct. *Stret* 4K **9**
Loire Clo. *Ash Z* 2K **25**
London Rd. *Coal* 1E **34**
Longbow Clo. *Stret* 5G **9**
Longbow Gro. *Stret* 5H **9**
Longcliff Rd. *Coal* 2J **35**
Longfellow Clo. *Burt T* 7J **9**
Longhedge La. *A'lw* 6D **8**
Longlands La. *Find* 4K **7**
Longlands Rd. *Mid* 1A **20**
Long La. *Coal* 7F **29**
Longmead Rd. *Burt T* 1H **13**
Long St. *Burt T* 1K **17**
Lonsdale Rd. *Bran* 7G **13**
Lords Clo. *Coal* 3H **35**
Lordswell Rd. *Burt T* 3D **12**
Loudoun Way. *Ash Z* 4J **25**
Loughborough Rd. *Cole* 2K **27**
Loughborough Rd. *Thri* 2E **28**
Loughborough Rd. *Whit* 3F **29**
Lount La. *A'lw* 5D **8**
Lovatt Clo. *Stret* 4A **10**
Lwr. Church St. *Ash Z* 3B **26**
Lwr. High St. *Tut* 6B **4**
Lwr. Moor Rd. *Cole* 1K **27**
Lwr. Outwoods Rd. *Burt T* 2E **12**
Lwr. Packington Rd. *Ash Z* 4A **26**
Loweswater Gro. *Ash Z* 5B **26**
Lucas La. *Hilt* 3K **5**
Ludgate St. *Tut* 7B **4**
Lullington M. *Over* 6H **23**
Lullington Rd. *Over* 6H **23**
Lyndham Av. *Burt T* 6A **14**
Lyne Ct. *Burt T* 4F **13**
Lynwood Clo. *Bran* 1E **16**
Lynwood Rd. *Bran* 1D **16**

M

McAdam Clo. *Stape* 5C **14**
McCarthy Clo. *Whit* 4F **29**
Mackworth Clo. *Newh* 1J **19**
Madras Rd. *Burt T* 4D **14**
Main Rd. *A'lw* 1A **12**
Main St. *Alb V* 7K **19**
Main St. *A'lw* 7B **8**
Main St. *B'dby* 1E **24**
Main St. *Bran* 1D **16**
Main St. *Burna* 1H **7**
Main St. *C'wll* 2A **22**
Main St. *Egg* 1C **10**
Main St. *Etw* 1C **6**
Main St. *Harts* 1E **20**
Main St. *Heat* 7H **33**
Main St. *Hilt* 3G **5**
Main St. *L'tn* 3D **22**
Main St. *Newh* 2F **19**
Main St. *Newt S* 6F **11**
Main St. *Norm H* 4E **32**
Main St. *Oakt* 3D **30**
Main St. *Over* 6J **23**
Main St. *R'stn* 2K **33**
Main St. *Rep* 5K **11**
Main St. *Smis* 5J **21**
Main St. *Stape* 7K **13**
Main St. *Stret* 5K **9**
Main St. *Swan* 3C **28**
Main St. *Swep* 7B **32**
Main St. *Tat* 7A **12**
Main St. *Thri* 1E **28**
Main St. *Walt T* 7B **16**
Mallard Clo. *Mea* 6E **30**
Malmesbury Av. *Mid* 2A **20**
Malthouse La. *Fos* 2C **4**
Maltings Ind. Est. *Burt T* 1K **13**
Maltings, The. *Burt T* 6B **14**
(Heritage Way)
Maltings, The. *Burt T* 3K **13**
(Wharf Rd.)
Malvern Av. *Burt T* 6A **14**
Malvern Cres. *Ash Z* 1K **25**
Malvern St. *Burt T* 6A **14**
Mammoth St. *Coal* 1E **34**
Manchester La. *Harts* 2E **20**
Mannings Ter. *Mea* 6F **31**
Mnr. Brook Clo. *Don H* 5D **34**
Manor Clo. *Ash Z* 4B **26**
Manor Clo. *Burt T* 2B **18**
Manor Cres. *Burt T* 2B **18**
Manor Cft. *Burt T* 5K **13**
Manor Dri. *Burt T* 5K **13**
Manor Rd. *Burt T* 2B **18**
Manor Rd. *Don H* 4C **34**
Mansfields Cft. *Etw* 1C **6**
Mantle La. *Coal* 7D **28**
Manton Clo. *Newh* 2G **19**
Maple Dri. *Ibs* 6A **34**
Maple Gro. *Burt T* 3K **17**
Maple Rd. *Mid* 2J **19**
Maple Way. *Bran* 7E **12**
Maplewell. *Coal* 1J **35**
Margaret St. *Coal* 1D **34**
Marigold Pl. *W'vle* 4C **20**
Market Pl. *Burt T* 5K **13**
Market Pl. *Whit* 4G **29**
Market St. *Ash Z* 3A **26**
Market St. *Chur G* 6J **19**
Market St. *Coal* 7D **28**
Market St. *Swad* 4J **19**
Marlborough Ct. *Coal* 1D **34**
Marlborough Cres. *Burt T* 7A **14**
Marlborough Sq. *Coal* 1D **34**
Marlborough Way. *Ash Z* 3K **25**
Marlow Dri. *Bran* 7F **13**
Marsden Clo. *R'stn* 7A **28**
Marston Brook. *Hilt* 4K **5**
Marston Clo. *Moi* 4D **24**
Marston La. *Hatt* 5C **4**
Marston La. *Rol D & Hilt* 2F **9**
Marston Old La. *Hatt* 5C **4**
Marston Ri. *Burt T* 7A **14**
Martin Clo. *Whit* 3E **28**
Maryland Ct. *Newh* 1H **19**
Masefield Av. *Mid* 2K **19**
Masefield Clo. *Mea* 7E **30**
Masefield Cres. *Burt T* 1J **13**
Matsyard Path. *Newh* 1G **19**
Matthews Clo. *Ash Z* 3J **25**
Mayfair. *Newh* 2F **19**
Mayfield Dri. *Burt T* 7B **14**
Mayfield Rd. *Burt T* 4B **14**
Maypole Hill. *Newh* 2H **19**
Mead Cres. *Burt T* 2B **18**
Meadow Ct. Burt T *4A* ***14***
(off Meadow Rd.)
Meadow Gdns. *Mea* 7F **31**
Meadow La. *Coal* 1H **35**
Meadow La. *Newh* 3G **19**
(in two parts)
Meadow La. *Stret* 6B **10**
Meadow Rd. *Burt T* 4A **14**
Meadowside Dri. *Burt T* 4K **13**
Meadowside Leisure Cen. **4K** 13
Meadow Vw. *Hug* 5D **34**
Meadow Vw. *Rol D* 2H **9**
Mdw. View Rd. *Newh* 3G **19**
Meadow Wlk. *Ibs* 6B **34**
Meadow Way. *Newh* 2H **19**
Mead Wlk. *Burt T* 2B **18**
Mear Greaves La. *Burt T* 3C **14**
Mease Clo. *Mea* 6F **31**
Mease, The. *Hilt* 4K **5**
Measham Rd. *Ash Z & Pack* 2J **31**
(in two parts)
Measham Rd. *Mea* 7C **30**
Measham Rd. *Moi & Doni* 6C **24**
(in two parts)
Measham Rd. *Oakt* 4A **30**
Melbourne Av. *Burt T* 4D **14**
Melbourne Rd. *Ibs* 5A **34**
Melbourne Rd. *R'stn* 6K **33**
Melbourne St. *Coal* 1D **34**
Mellor Rd. *Bran* 1F **17**
Melrose Clo. *Ash Z* 3C **26**
Melrose Rd. *Thri* 1E **28**
Melville Ct. *Etw* 2C **6**
Memorial Sq. *Coal* 1D **34**
Mendip Clo. *Ash Z* 4A **26**
Mercia Clo. *Hatt* 5C **4**
Mercia Dri. *Will* 1H **11**
Meredith Clo. *Burt T* 1J **13**
Mereoak La. *B'dby* 1H **21**
Merganster Way. *Coal* 2H **35**
Merlin Cres. *Bran* 7E **12**
Merlin Way. *W'vle* 5C **20**
Merrydale Rd. *Burt T* 7A **14**
Mervyn Rd. *Burt T* 4B **14**
Mewies Clo. *Walt T* 7C **16**
Mews, The. *Burt T* 1H **17**
Meynell Clo. *Burt T* 6C **14**
Meynell St. *Chur G* 7H **19**
Mickleden Grn. *Whit* 7H **29**
Mickleton Clo. *Chur G* 7J **19**
Middle Clo. *Swad* 4J **19**
Midland Grain Warehouse. Burt T *4H* ***13***
(off Derby St.)
Midland Rd. *Hug & Elli* 5D **34**
Midland Rd. *Swad* 3J **19**
(in two parts)
Midway Rd. *Mid* 3K **19**
Midway Rd. *Swad* 3K **19**
Mill Bank. *Ash Z* 3A **26**
Mill Clo. *Find* 3K **7**
Mill Clo. *Mid* 3K **19**
Mill Clo. *Newt S* 6F **11**
Mill Dam. *Hug* 4E **34**
Millersdale Clo. *Burt T* 2C **14**
Millers La. *Burt T* 4H **13**

Millfield Clo. *Ash Z* 1K **25**
Millfield Cft. *Mid* 1J **19**
Millfield St. *W'vle* 6D **20**
Mill Fleam. *Hilt* 4K **5**
Mill Hill Dri. *Burt T* 3C **14**
Mill Hill La. *Burt T* 3B **14**
Mill La. *Ash Z* 3A **26**
Mill La. *Heat* 7H **33**
Mill La. *Hilt* 3H **5**
Mill La. *Swan* 2B **28**
Mill Mdw. Way. *Etw* 1C **6**
Mill Pond. *Hug* 4E **34**
Millpool Clo. *Harts* 1D **20**
Mill St. *Pack* 7A **26**
Milton Av. *Mid* 2K **19**
Milton Clo. *Mea* 7F **31**
Milton Ho. Burt T *4H* ***13***
(off Cross St.)
Milton Rd. *Rep* 3K **11**
Milton St. *Burt T* 5H **13**
Milward La. *Burna* 1H **7**
Miry La. *Chur B* 1B **4**
Mitre Dri. *Rep* 4K **11**
Moat Bank. *Bret* 5E **14**
Moat St. *Chur G* 7J **19**
Moira Furnace Mus. **6B** 24
Moira Rd. *Ash Z & Shell* 3F **25**
Moira Rd. *Doni* 1C **30**
Moira Rd. *Over* 6J **23**
Moira Rd. *W'vle* 2A **24**
Monarch Clo. *Stret* 6K **9**
Mona Rd. *Burt T* 2G **13**
Money Hill. *Ash Z* 1A **26**
Monk St. *Tut* 7B **4**
Monsaldale Clo. *Burt T* 3C **14**
Monsom La. *Rep* 3K **11**
Montgomery Clo. *Hilt* 3K **5**
Montpelier Clo. *Burt T* 1F **17**
Moores Clo. *Burt T* 1G **13**
Moor Furlong. *Stret* 5A **10**
Moorlands, The. *Cole* 6J **27**
Moor La. *Cole* 3K **27**
Moor Rd. *Elli* 7F **35**
Moor St. *Burt T* 5H **13**
(in two parts)
Moor, The. *Cole* 2K **27**
Morley's Hill. *Burt T* 7G **9**
Morrisons Retail Pk. *Coal* 7E **28**
Morton Wlk. *Ash Z* 5J **25**
Mosley M., The. *Rol D* 2F **9**
Mosley St. *Burt T* 5H **13**
Mossdale. *Whit* 3F **29**
Mountbatten Clo. *Stret* 6J **9**
Mt. Pleasant Rd. *Cas G* 1F **23**
Mt. Pleasant Rd. *Chur G* 7H **19**
Mount Rd. *Bret* 4H **15**
Mount Rd. *Cas G* 1E **22**
Mount Rd. *Harts* 4D **20**
Mount St. *Burt T* 4B **14**
Mount Wlk. *Ash Z* 3B **26**
Mulberry Way. *Hilt* 3K **5**
Muscovey Rd. *Coal* 2H **35**
Mushroom La. *Alb V* 7K **19**
Musson Dri. *Ash Z* 4K **25**

N

Nankirk La. *A'lw* 2A **12**
Napier St. *Burt T* 6H **13**
Narrow La. *Doni* 2B **30**
Naseby Dri. *Ash Z* 2C **26**
Nature Reserve. **2E** 16
Navigation St. *Mea* 5F **31**
Needhams Wlk. *Coal* 1E **34**
Needwood Ct. *Tut* 7B **4**
Needwood St. *Burt T* 4G **13**
Nelson Fields. *Coal* 7H **29**
Nelson Pl. *Smis* 5J **21**
Nelson St. *Burt T* 4D **14**
Nelson St. *Swad* 3J **19**
Nene Clo. *Stret* 5H **9**
Nene Way. *Coal* 3H **35**
Nene Way. *Hilt* 4J **5**
Netherclose La. *Hatt* 4A **4**
Nethercroft Dri. *Pack* 7B **26**
Nether Hall La. *Harts* 1A **20**
Neville Clo. *Rol D* 3G **9**
Neville Dri. *Coal* 1H **35**
New Broadway Shop. Cen. *Coal* 1D **34**
Newbury Dri. *Stret* 5H **9**
Newby Clo. *Burt T* 6C **14**
New Clo. *Swan* 5B **28**
Newfield Rd. *Burt T* 3C **14**
Newgatefield La. *A'lw* 6C **8**
Newhall Rd. *Swad* 3J **19**
Newhay. *Stret* 5A **10**
Newlands Clo. *Chur G* 6H **19**
Newman Dri. *Bran* 7G **13**
Newport Clo. *Burt T* 7J **9**
New Rd. *Cole* 1B **28**
New Rd. *Hilt* 3K **5**
New Rd. *Newh* 2F **19**
(in two parts)
New Rd. *W'vle* 6C **20**
New Row. *Ibs* 7B **34**
New St. *Burt T* 5J **13**
New St. *Chur G* 6J **19**
New St. *Coal* 2E **34**
New St. *Doni* 1B **30**
New St. *Hug* 3C **34**
New St. *Mea* 4E **30**
New St. *Oakt* 3D **30**
Newton Clo. *Newt S* 6F **11**
Newton La. *Bret* 6F **11**
Newton Leys. *Burt T* 3D **14**
Newton M. *Burt T* 4A **14**
Newton Pk. Clo. *Newh* 1H **19**
Newton Rd. *Burt T & Newt S* 4A **14**
Nicklaus Clo. *Bran* 1F **17**
Nicolson Way. *Burt T* 6F **13**
Nightingale Dri. *W'vle* 5C **20**
Ninelands Mobile Home Pk. *Harts* 4D **20**
Ninth Av. *Burt T* 7D **12**
Norfolk Rd. *Burt T* 2J **17**
Normandy Rd. *Hilt* 3K **5**
Norman Keep. *Tut* 7B **4**
Norman Rd. *Tut* 7B **4**
Normanton La. *Heat* 6G **33**
Normanton La. *Norm H* 4C **32**
Normanton Rd. *Pack & Norm H* 1B **32**
Norris Hill. *Moi* 3E **24**
North Av. *Coal* 3E **34**
North Clo. *B'dby* 1E **24**
North Clo. *Will* 1J **11**
Northfield Dri. *Coal* 2H **35**
Northfield Rd. *Burt T* 7H **9**
Northfields. *Ash Z* 1A **26**
Northside Bus. Pk. *Burt T* 1K **13**
North St. *Ash Z* 3A **26**
North St. *Burt T* 4C **14**
North St. *Swad* 3J **19**
North St. *Whit* 4F **29**
Northumberland Rd. *Burt T* 1J **17**
North Wlk. *Mea* 3G **31**
Norton Rd. *Burt T* 1F **13**
Nottingham Rd. *Ash Z* 2B **26**
Nottingham Rd. *Cole* 1B **28**
Nottingham Rd. Ind. Est. *Ash Z* 2C **26**
Nursery Clo. *Swad* 2J **19**

O

Oadby Ri. *Burt T* 1F **13**
Oak Clo. *Cas G* 2F **23**
Oak Clo. *Coal* 2H **35**
Oak Clo. *Mea* 5F **31**
Oak Dri. *Hilt* 3J **5**
Oak Dri. *Ibs* 7A **34**
Oakham Dri. *Coal* 7K **29**
Oakham Gro. *Ash Z* 2K **25**
Oaklands Rd. *Etw* 1D **6**
Oakleigh Av. *Newh* 3G **19**
Oakleigh Ct. *Ash Z* 3A **26**
Oaks Ind. Est. *Coal* 1B **34**
Oak Sq. *Chur G* 6G **19**
Oaks Rd. *Whit* 3H **29**
Oaks Rd. *Will* 1J **11**
Oak St. *Burt T* 6G **13**
Oak St. *Chur G* 6H **19**
Oak Tree Rd. *Hug* 3C **34**
Oakwood Clo. *Hatt* 5B **4**
Occupation La. *W'vle* 7A **20**
Occupation Rd. *Alb V* 2J **23**
Octagon Cen., The. *Burt T* 5J **13**
Oldfield Dri. *Swad* 3K **19**
Oldfield La. *Hilt* 5A **6**
Old Hall Dri. *Will* 1J **11**
Old Hall Gdns. *Chur G* 6H **19**
Oldicote La. *Bret* 4F **15**
Old Nurseries, The. *R'stn* 2A **34**
Old Parks La. *Smis* 6K **21**
Old Rd. *Bran* 1D **16**
Old School Clo. *Elli* 7E **34**
Old Sta. Clo. *Coal* 1E **34**
Old Toll Ga. *W'vle* 5B **20**
Orchard Clo. *Hilt* 4J **5**
Orchard Clo. *R'stn* 7A **28**
Orchard Clo. *Walt T* 7C **16**
Orchard Clo. *Will* 7J **7**
Orchard Pk. *Burt T* 5J **13**
Orchard St. *Burt T* 6J **13**
Orchard St. *Ibs* 7B **34**
Orchard St. *Newh* 2G **19**
Orchard Way. *Mea* 5F **31**
Orchid Clo. *Burt T* 7B **14**
Ordish Ct. *Burt T* 5J **13**
Ordish St. *Burt T* 5H **13**
Ortons Ind. Est. *Coal* 1E **34**
Osborne Ct. *Burt T* 1G **13**
Osborne St. *Burt T* 4B **14**
Osprey Clo. *Burt T* 3E **14**
Oundle Clo. *Ash Z* 1J **25**
Outfield Rd. *Burt T* 7A **14**
Outwoods Clo. Burt T *1F* ***13***
(off Lwr. Outwoods Rd.)
Outwoods La. *A'lw & Burt T* 7B **8**
(in three parts)
Outwoods La. *Cole* 1K **27**
Outwoods St. *Burt T* 2G **13**
Oval, The. *Coal* 3H **35**
Oversetts Ct. *Newh* 2G **19**
Oversetts Rd. *Newh* 3F **19**
(in two parts)
Overton Clo. *Cole* 2K **27**
Owen's Bank. *Tut* 7A **4**
Owen St. *Coal* 1D **34**
Oxford St. *Burt T* 6G **13**
Oxford St. *Chur G* 7H **19**
Oxford St. *Coal* 1F **35**
Ox Hey Pleasure Ground. **6K** 13
Oxley Rd. *Burt T* 4B **14**

P

Packington Nook La. *Ash Z* 5K **25**
Paddocks, The. *New H* 3G **19**
Paddock, The. *Burt T* 3C **14**
Paddock, The. *Rol D* 2F **9**
Paget Rd. *Ibs* 5B **34**
Paget St. *Burt T* 5H **13**
Palmer Clo. *Bran* 7G **13**
Paradise Clo. *Moi* 5D **24**
Pares Clo. *Whit* 4F **29**
Paris Clo. *Ash Z* 2K **25**
Parish Church of St Modwen, The. **5K** 13
Park Av. *Chur B* 1A **4**
Park Clo. *Ash Z* 5K **25**
Park Clo. *L'tn* 3D **22**
Park Ct. *Swad* 3K **19**
Parkdale. *Ibs* 7A **34**
Parkers Clo. *B'dby* 1E **24**
Parker St. *Burt T* 2J **13**
Park La. *Tut* 7A **4**
Park Pale, The. *Tut* 1B **8**
Park Rd. *Ash Z* 2A **26**
Park Rd. *Chur G* 6J **19**
Park Rd. *Coal* 1E **34**
Park Rd. *Moi* 7B **24**
Park Rd. *Over* 3G **23**
Park Rd. *Stant* 4D **18**
Park St. *Burt T* 5H **13**
(in two parts)
Park St. *Newh* 2H **19**
Park Vw. *Whit* 4F **29**
Parkway. *Burt T* 7D **12**
Park Way. *Etw* 1D **6**
Parliament St. *Newh* 2G **19**

Parsons Clo. *Chur G* 7H **19**
Parsonwood Hill. *Whit* 3F **29**
Partridge Dri. *W'vle* 5C **20**
Pastures La. *Oakt* 3E **30**
Pastures, The. *New H* 3G **19**
Pastures, The. *Rep* 4K **11**
Patch Clo. *Burt T* 1G **13**
Patrick Clo. *L'tn* 4E **22**
Paulyn Way. *Ash Z* 4J **25**
Peacroft Ct. *Hilt* 3J **5**
Peacroft La. *Hilt* 3J **5**
Peartree Av. *Newh* 1G **19**
Pear Tree Clo. *Harts* 1D **20**
Pear Tree Ct. *Etw* 1C **6**
Pear Tree Dri. *L'tn* 3D **22**
Peel St. *Burt T* 6H **13**
Pegasus Way. *Hilt* 3K **5**
Pegg's Clo. *Mea* 5F **31**
Peggs Grange. *Hug* 4E **34**
Peldar Pl. *Coal* 2J **35**
Penistone St. *Ibs* 6B **34**
Penkridge Rd. *Chur G* 7J **19**
Pennine Way. *Ash Z* 4A **26**
Pennine Way. *Swad* 5H **19**
Pensgreave Rd. *Burt T* 1G **13**
Pentland Rd. *Ash Z* 3C **26**
Percy Wood Clo. *Hilt* 3H **5**
Peregrine Clo. *Burt T* 4E **14**
Peregrine Clo. *Mea* 6F **31**
Perran Av. *Whit* 7H **29**
Pershore Dri. *Bran* 7F **13**
Perth Clo. *Burt T* 5D **14**
Peterfield Rd. *Whit* 6H **29**
Peters Ct. *Hatt* 4C **4**
Pickering Dri. *Elli* 6D **34**
Piddocks Rd. *Stant* 3C **18**
(in two parts)
Pine Clo. *Ash Z* 2C **26**
Pine Clo. *Bran* 7F **13**
Pine Clo. *Etw* 1D **6**
Pine Gro. *Newh* 2G **19**
Pines, The. *Whit* 6H **29**
Pine Wlk. *Cas G* 2F **23**
Pinewood Rd. *Burt T* 2A **18**
Pinfold Clo. *Tut* 1B **8**
Pingle Farm Rd. *Newh* 3G **19**
Pintail Ct. Mea *6E* ***30***
(off Widgeon Dri.)
Piper La. *R'stn* 1A **34**
Pipit Clo. *Mea* 6F **31**
Pisca La. *Heat* 7H **33**
Pithiviers Clo. *Ash Z* 4K **25**
Pitt La. *Cole* 3K **27**
Plover Av. *W'vle* 5C **20**
Plummer Rd. *Newh* 2G **19**
Pollard Way. *R'stn* 7B **28**
Pool St. *Chur G* 6A **20**
Poplar Av. *Mid* 2J **19**
Poplar Av. *Moi* 7B **24**
Poplar Dri. *Mea* 4F **31**
Poplars Rd. *Burt T* 7H **9**
Porter's La. *Find* 3K **7**
(in two parts)
Portland Av. *Burt T* 1F **17**
Portland St. *Etw* 1C **6**
Portway Dri. *Tut* 1B **8**
Postern Rd. *Tat* 3A **12**
Potlocks, The. *Will* 7K **7**
Potters Cft. *Swad* 3H **19**
Prentice Clo. *Moi* 5D **24**
Preston's La. *Cole* 3K **27**
Prestop Dri. *Ash Z* 2J **25**
Prestwood Pk. Dri. *Mid* 3K **19**
Pretoria Rd. *Ibs* 6C **34**
Price Ct. *Burt T* 3E **12**
(in two parts)
Primrose Bank. *Etw* 1D **6**
Primrose Dri. *Bran* 7F **13**
Primrose Mdw. *Mid* 1J **19**
Princess Av. *L'tn* 4D **22**
Princess Clo. *W'vle* 6C **20**
Princess St. *Burt T* 3H **13**
Princess St. *Cas G* 1G **23**
Princess Way. *Stret* 6K **9**
Prince St. *Coal* 2E **34**
Priorfields. *Ash Z* 4B **26**
(in two parts)
Prior Pk. Ash Z *4B* ***26***
(off Up. Packington Rd.)
Prior Pk. Rd. *Ash Z* 3A **26**
Priory Clo. *Newh* 2H **19**
Priory Clo. *Thri* 1D **28**
Priory Clo. *Tut* 1A **8**
Priory Lands. *Stret* 4K **9**
Provident Ct. *W'vle* 6C **20**

Q

Queens Ct. *Bran* 7G **13**
Queens Dri. *Swad* 2J **19**
QUEENS HOSPITAL. 2F **13**
Queensland Cres. *Burt T* 5D **14**
Queens Ri. *Tut* 7B **4**
Queen's St. *Mea* 5F **31**
Queen St. *Burt T* 6H **13**
Queen St. *Chur G* 7H **19**
Queen St. *Coal* 2E **34**
Queensway Houses. *Mea* 5F **31**
Quelch Clo. *Hug* 4E **34**
Quorn Clo. *Burt T* 6B **14**
Quorn Cres. *Coal* 2J **35**

R

Radley Clo. *Ash Z* 1K **25**
Raglan Clo. *Stret* 6J **9**
Rambler Clo. *Newh* 3H **19**
Ramscliff Av. *Doni* 2C **30**
Randall Dri. *Swad* 4J **19**
Rangemore St. *Burt T* 4G **13**
Range Rd. *Ash Z* 3B **26**
Ratcliff Clo. *Ash Z* 3K **25**
Ratcliffe Av. *Bran* 7G **13**
Raven Clo. *Mea* 6E **30**
Ravenslea. *R'stn* 2K **33**
Ravenstone Rd. *Coal* 7B **28**
Ravenstone Rd. *Heat* 7H **33**
Ravenstone Rd. *Ibs* 7K **33**
Ravens Way. *Burt T* 3G **13**
Rawdon Rd. *Moi* 4B **24**
Rawdon Side. *Swad* 4A **20**
Red Burrow La. *Norm H & Pack* 2B **32**
Red Hill La. *Swan & Thri* 4C **28**
Redhill La. *Tut* 1A **8**
Redhill Lodge Rd. *Newh* 1H **19**
Redlands Est. *Ibs* 5C **34**
Redmoor Clo. *Burt T* 4C **14**
Redwood Dri. *Burt T* 7B **14**
Reform Rd. *Ibs* 7B **34**
Regan Rd. *Moi* 5D **24**
Regency Way. *Stret* 6J **9**
Regent Ct. *Chur G* 6J **19**
Regents Pk. Rd. *Bran* 1F **17**
Regent St. *Chur G* 7H **19**
Regs Way. *Bar H* 4J **35**
Rempstone Rd. *Cole & Grif* 2H **27**
Rennes Clo. *Ash Z* 3K **25**
Renshaw Dri. *Newh* 3G **19**
Repton Clo. *Ash Z* 1K **25**
Repton Rd. *Harts* 1B **20**
Repton Rd. *Mea* 5D **30**
Repton Rd. *Newt S* 6F **11**
Repton Rd. *Will* 1H **11**
Reservoir Hill. *Alb V & Moi* 2A **24**
Reservoir Rd. *Burt T* 3E **12**
Resolution Rd. *Ash Z* 2C **26**
Rest Haven. *Swad* 3J **19**
Richmond Ct. *Rep* 4K **11**
Richmond Rd. *Ibs & Don H* 5D **34**
Richmond St. *Burt T* 3H **13**
Ricknild St. *Bran* 7E **12**
Ridgeway Rd. *Burt T* 2K **17**
Ridgway Rd. *Ash Z* 4K **25**
Rink Dri. *Swad* 5J **19**
Risborrow Clo. *Etw* 1F **7**
Rise, The. *Newh* 3G **19**
River Bank, The. *Will* 1J **11**
Riverdale Clo. *Burt T* 2C **14**
River Sence Way. *Hug* 4E **34**
Riverside. *Walt T* 7B **16**
Riverside Cvn. Pk. *Burt T* 1A **14**
Riverside Cen., The. *Burt T* 4K **13**
Riverside Ct. *Mea* 6D **30**
Riverside Dri. *Bran* 2E **16**
Robian Way. *Swad* 4H **19**
Robin Hood Pl. *Chur G* 6K **19**
Robin Rd. *Coal* 2G **35**
Robinson Rd. *Newh* 2G **19**
Robinson Rd. *Whit* 4E **28**
Rochdale Cres. *Coal* 1K **35**
Rockcliffe Clo. *Chur G* 7J **19**
Rockingham Clo. *Ash Z* 4B **26**
Rockland Ri. *Whit* 3G **29**
Roedean Clo. *Ash Z* 2K **25**
Rolleston La. *Tut* 1C **8**
Rolleston Rd. *Stret & Burt T* 5G **9**
Romans Cres. *Coal* 1K **35**
Rookery, The. *Heat* 7G **33**
Rope Wlk., The. *Burt T* 6H **13**
Rose Av. *Stret* 4B **10**
Rose Cottage Clo. *Burt T* 6H **13**
Rose Cottage Gdns. *Burt T* 6J **13**
Rosecroft Gdns. *Swad* 6J **19**
Rosedale. *Whit* 2F **29**
Rose Hill. *W'vle* 5B **20**
Roseleigh Cres. *Newh* 2G **19**
Rosemary Cres. *Whit* 5H **29**
Rosemount Rd. *Burt T* 5A **14**
Rose Tree La. *Newh* 1G **19**
Rose Valley. *Newh* 3H **19**
Rosewood Rd. *Burt T* 2A **18**
Rosliston Rd. *Burt T* 2K **17**
Rosliston Rd. *C'wll & Drake* 7H **17**
Rosliston Rd. *Walt T* 7C **16**
Rosliston Rd. S. *Burt T & Drake* 3K **17**
Rossall Dri. *Ash Z* 2K **25**
Rosslyn Rd. *Whit* 5G **29**
Rotherwood Dri. *Ash Z* 2A **26**
Rouen Way. *Ash Z* 3K **25**
Rowan Av. *Coal* 2J **35**
Rowan Clo. *Mea* 4F **31**
Rowan Clo. *Moi* 3E **24**
Rowan Dri. *Ibs* 7A **34**
Rowbury Dri. *Burt T* 5C **14**
Rowena Dri. *Ash Z* 2A **26**
Rowlands, The. *Cole* 4K **27**
Rowley Clo. *Swad* 3A **20**
Rowley Ct. *Swad* 4J **19**
Rowton St. *Burt T* 7G **9**
Rugby Clo. *Ash Z* 1K **25**
Rugby Clo. *Burt T* 7H **13**
Rumsey Clo. *Thri* 1D **28**
Rushby Rd. *Elli* 7F **35**
Rushton Clo. *Tut* 7B **4**
Ruskin Pl. *Burt T* 1J **13**
Russell St. *Burt T* 5J **13**
Russell St. *Swad* 5K **19**
Russet Clo. *Hatt* 4B **4**
Ruston Clo. *Swad* 4J **19**
Rutland Clo. *Burt T* 2J **17**
Rydal Gdns. *Ash Z* 5B **26**
Ryder Clo. *Swad* 5E **18**
Ryeflatts La. *Hatt* 4C **4**
Ryknild Trad. Est. *Burt T* 1K **13**

S

Sage Dri. *W'vle* 4C **20**
St Aidan's Clo. *Burt T* 7H **9**
St Albans Ct. *Burt T* 7H **9**
St Andrew's Clo. *Thri* 1E **28**
St Andrew's Dri. *Burt T* 6H **9**
St Bernard's Rd. *Whit* 5G **29**
St Catherine's Rd. *Newh* 3G **19**
St Chad's Clo. *Burt T* 6H **9**
St Chad's Rd. *Burt T* 7H **9**
St Christophers Pk. Homes. *Elli* 7F **35**
St Christopher's Rd. *Elli* 7F **35**
St Clares Ct. *Coal* 2F **35**
St David's Ct. *Coal* 1K **35**
St David's Cres. *Coal* 7K **29**
St David's Dri. *Burt T* 6H **9**
St Denys' Cres. *Ibs* 7A **34**
St Edwards Ct. *Newh* 3G **19**
St Faiths Rd. *Coal* 3D **34**
St Francis Clo. *Burt T* 6J **9**
St George's Hill. *Swan* 2B **28**
St Georges Rd. *Burt T* 2E **12**

St Ives. *Coal* 2J **35**
St James Clo. *Will* 1K **11**
St John's Clo. *Heat* 7G **33**
St John's Clo. *Hug* 4E **34**
St John's Ct. *Burt T* 7H **9**
St John's Dri. *Newh* 3F **19**
St John's Rd. *Burt T* 7H **9**
St Jude's Way. *Burt T* 6H **9**
St Luke's Rd. *Burt T* 6H **9**
St Margarets. *Burt T* 2E **12**
St Marks Rd. *Burt T* 6H **9**
St Martin's Clo. *Burt T* 6G **9**
St Mary's Av. *Don H* 4C **34**
St Mary's Clo. *Newt S* 6F **11**
St Mary's Ct. *Don H* 4C **34**
St Mary's Dri. *Burt T* 6H **9**
St Mary's Dri. *Stret* 4A **10**
St Mary's La. *Coal* 3A **34**
St Matthew's St. *Burt T* 7H **13**
St Michael's Clo. *Ash Z* 4B **26**
St Michael's Clo. *Will* 1J **11**
St Michaels' Dri. *R'stn* 2K **33**
St Michaels Rd. *Burt T* 6J **9**
St Modwen's Clo. *Burt T* 7H **9**
St Modwen's Wlk. *Burt T* 5J **13**
St Patricks Rd. *Burt T* 6H **9**
St Paul's Ct. *Burt T* 4G **13**
St Paul's Sq. *Burt T* 3G **13**
St Paul's St. W. *Burt T* 3G **13**
St Peter's Bri. *Burt T* 6J **13**
St Peter's Ct. *Burt T* 6A **14**
St Peters Retail Pk. *Burt T* 6J **13**
St Peter's St. *Burt T* 6A **14**
St Saviours Rd. *Coal* 2D **34**
St Stephens Ct. *Burt T* 7H **9**
St Stephen's Ct. *W'vle* 5C **20**
St Vincents Clo. *Coal* 3D **34**
Sales La. *Burt T* 4D **14**
Salisbury Av. *Burt T* 4D **14**
Salisbury Dri. *Mid* 2B **20**
Saltersford Valley Picnic Area. **2C 30**
Samson Rd. *Coal* 7E **28**
Sandalwood Rd. *Burt T* 2K **17**
Sandcliffe Pk. *Mid* 1A **20**
Sandcliffe Rd. *Mid* 2A **20**
Sandcroft Clo. *Mid* 3A **20**
Sandford Brook. *Hilt* 4K **5**
Sandhills Clo. *Mea* 6F **31**
Sandhole La. *Whit* 1K **29**
Sandlands, The. *Mid* 2A **20**
Sandown Clo. *Bran* 1F **17**
Sandringham Av. *Burt T* 6B **14**
Sandringham Rd. *Coal* 2G **35**
Sandtop Clo. *B'dby* 1E **24**
Sandtop La. *B'dby* 1E **24**
Sandy La. *C'wll* 2A **22**
Sandypits La. *Etw* 1D **6**
(in two parts)
Sawpit La. *Hatt* 3B **4**
Saxon Clo. *Burt T* 1A **18**
Saxon Gro. *Will* 1H **11**
Saxon St. *Burt T* 1A **18**
Saxon Way. *Ash Z* 2K **25**
Scalpcliffe Clo. *Burt T* 5A **14**
Scalpcliffe Rd. *Burt T* 4A **14**
School Clo. *Alb V* 7K **19**
School La. *Cole* 1B **28**
School La. *Norm H* 4E **32**
School La. *Rol D* 2G **9**
School La. *Whit* 3E **28**
School M. *Hatt* 4C **4**
School St. *Chur G* 6J **19**
School St. *Moi* 7C **24**
School St. *Oakt* 3D **30**
Scotlands Dri. *Coal* 2E **34**
Scotlands Ind. Est. *Coal* 2F **35**
Scotlands Rd. *Coal* 2E **34**
Scott Clo. *Ash Z* 2K **25**
Scotts, The. *Cas G* 1E **22**
Scropton Old Rd. *Hatt* 5B **4**
Scropton Rd. *Hatt* 4A **4**
Seagrave Clo. *Coal* 1K **35**
Sealey Clo. *Will* 1K **11**
Seals Rd. *Doni* 1B **30**
Seal Vw. *L'tn* 3D **22**
Sealwood La. *L'tn* 4E **22**
Second Av. *Burt T* 6D **12**
Sedgefield Rd. *Bran* 1E **16**
Sefton Clo. *Burt T* 6C **14**
Seventh Av. *Burt T* 6E **12**
Severn Clo. *Stret* 5H **9**
Severn Dri. *Burt T* 4K **13**
Seymour Av. *Burt T* 7K **9**
Shackland Dri. *Mea* 5G **31**
Shady Gro. *Hilt* 3H **5**
Shaef Clo. *Hilt* 3K **5**
Shakespeare Clo. *Swad* 2K **19**
Shakespeare Rd. *Burt T* 1H **13**
Shannon App. *Burt T* 5J **13**
Sharpley Av. *Coal* 7H **29**
Sharpswood Mnr. *W'vle* 4B **20**
Sheffield St. *Burt T* 6H **13**
Shellbrook Clo. *Shell* 3H **25**
Shelley Av. *Burt T* 1J **13**
Shelley Clo. *Burt T* 1J **13**
Shelley Clo. *Mea* 7F **31**
Shelley Rd. *Swad* 3K **19**
Sherbourne Dri. *Ash Z* 2K **25**
Sherbourne Dri. *Burt T* 1F **17**
Sherman Clo. *Hilt* 3K **5**
Sherwood Clo. *Elli* 6E **34**
Shieling, The. *Hatt* 3B **4**
Shipley Clo. *Bran* 7G **13**
Shire Horse Stables. **4J 13**
Shobnall Clo. *Burt T* 3G **13**
Shobnall Ct. *Burt T* 4G **13**
Shobnall Fields Recreation Ground. **3F 13**
Shobnall Leisure Complex. **3F 13**
Shobnall Rd. *Burt T* 3E **12**
Shobnall St. *Burt T* 4G **13**
Shortheath. *Over* 6K **23**
Shortheath Rd. *Moi* 6A **24**
Short St. *Burt T* 1K **17**
Shotwoodhill La. *Rol D* 1E **8**
Shrewsbury Rd. *Stret* 4A **10**
Shrewsbury Wlk. *Thri* 1E **28**
Shrubbery, The. *W'vle* 6D **20**
Siddalls St. *Burt T* 4C **14**
Sidings Ind. Est. *Burt T* 3K **13**
Silk Mill La. *Tut* 7B **4**
Silkstone Clo. *Chur G* 7J **19**
Silverhill Clo. *Stret* 5H **9**
Silver St. *Oakt* 4D **30**
Silver St. *Whit* 5F **29**
Sinai Clo. *Burt T* 3E **12**
Siskin Dri. *Mea* 6E **30**
Ski Cen. **5K 19**
Skinner's La. *Whit* 4G **29**
Skylark Clo. *Mea* 6E **30**
Slackey La. *Moi* 5K **23**
Slack La. *Harts* 2E **20**
Slade Clo. *Etw* 1D **6**
Slaybarns Way. *Ibs* 6B **34**
Small Thorn Pl. *W'vle* 6C **20**
Smedley Clo. *Ash Z* 4J **25**
Smedley Ct. *Egg* 1C **10**
Smisby Rd. *Ash Z* 6K **21**
Smith Ct. *Whit* 4E **28**
Smith Cres. *Coal* 1K **35**
Smithy La. *Ash Z* 2D **26**
Snibston Discovery Pk. **1C 34**
Snibston Dri. *Coal* 7B **28**
Snipe Clo. *Coal* 1D **34**
Snipe Clo. *Hug* 3C **34**
Solney Clo. *Swad* 5G **19**
Somerset Rd. *Burt T* 2J **17**
Sorrel Dri. *W'vle* 4B **20**
S. Broadway St. *Burt T* 7H **13**
South Clo. *B'dby* 1E **24**
South Dri. *Newh* 2G **19**
South Hill. *Rol D* 2J **9**
South La. *Bar H* 6K **35**
S. Leicester Ind. Est. *Elli* 6F **35**
S. Oak St. *Burt T* 7G **13**
South St. *Ash Z* 3A **26**
South St. *Elli* 6E **34**
(in two parts)
South St. *W'vle* 7C **20**
S. Uxbridge St. *Burt T* 7G **13**
Sovereign Dri. *Bran* 7G **13**
Speedwell Clo. *Coal* 1F **35**
Speedwell Clo. *W'vle* 4C **20**
Spencer Clo. *Stret* 5J **9**
Spinney Clo. Ash Z *4A* ***26***
(off Stuart Way)
Spinney Lodge. *Rep* 4K **11**
Spinney Rd. *Bran* 7E **12**
Spinney, The. *Hug* 4D **34**
Spring Clo. *Cas G* 7H **19**
Spring Cottage Rd. *Over* 5K **23**
Springfarm Rd. *Burt T* 6B **14**
Springfield. *Thri* 1F **29**
Springfield Clo. *Ibs* 7B **34**
Springfield Clo. *Mid* 2J **19**
Springfield Rd. *Etw* 2C **6**
Springfield Rd. *Swad & Mid* 3J **19**
Springfield Vs. *Burt T* 6B **14**
Springhill. *Harts* 1D **20**
Spring La. *Pack* 7B **26**
Spring La. *Swan & Coal* 5C **28**
Spring Rd. *Ibs* 6C **34**
Spring St. *Cas G* 1H **23**
Spring Ter. Rd. *Burt T* 6A **14**
Springwood Farm Rd. *Mid* 1J **19**
Square, The. *Bret* 4J **15**
Square, The. *Oakt* 3D **30**
Squirrel Wlk. *Over* 6J **23**
Stafford St. *Burt T* 2J **13**
Stainsdale Grn. *Whit* 7H **29**
Staley Av. *Ash Z* 5J **25**
Stamford Dri. *Coal* 7K **29**
Stamps Clo. *Burt T* 4D **14**
Standard Hill. *Coal* 3C **34**
Standing Butts Clo. *Walt T* 7C **16**
Stanhope Glade. *Bret* 7H **15**
Stanhope Grn. *Bret* 6F **15**
Stanhope Rd. *Swad* 5J **19**
Stanhope St. *Burt T* 4C **14**
Stanleigh Rd. *Over* 5J **23**
Stanley Clo. *W'vle* 5C **20**
Stanley St. *Burt T* 5H **13**
Stanley St. *Swad* 4K **19**
Stanton Rd. *Burt T* 7A **14**
Stapenhill Rd. *Burt T* 6A **14**
Station Dri. *Moi* 5C **24**
Station Hill. *Swan* 5B **28**
Station La. *Walt T* 7B **16**
Station M. *Ash Z* 4A **26**
Station Rd. *Ash Z* 4A **26**
Station Rd. *Bar N* 7A **16**
Station Rd. *Hatt & Fos* 5B **4**
Station Rd. *Hug* 5D **34**
Station Rd. *Ibs* 7A **34**
Station Rd. *Rol D* 2G **9**
Station Rd. *W'vle* 6C **20**
Station St. *Burt T* 4H **13**
(in two parts)
Station St. *Cas G* 1G **23**
Station Wlk. *Stret* 5K **9**
Stenson Rd. *Coal* 7E **28**
Stephenson Ind. Est. *Coal* 7B **28**
Stephenson Way. *Coal* 6B **28**
Stephens Rd. *Bran* 7G **13**
Stewart Clo. *Bran* 2F **17**
Stinson Way. *Whit* 4E **28**
Stirling Ri. *Stret* 6J **9**
Stonehaven Clo. *Coal* 1K **35**
Stone Row. *Coal* 7E **28**
Stoneydale Clo. *Newh* 3G **19**
Stoney La. *Cole* 2K **27**
Stour Clo. *Hilt* 5K **5**
Stowe Clo. *Ash Z* 2K **25**
Strathmore Clo. *Coal* 2K **35**
Strawberry La. *B'dby* 1E **24**
Stretton Dri. *Coal* 1K **35**
Stretton Vw. *Oakt* 4C **30**
Stuart Way. *Ash Z* 4A **26**
Suffolk Rd. *Burt T* 2J **17**
Sunningdale Clo. *Stret* 5H **9**
Sunnyside. *Ibs* 7A **34**
Sunnyside. *Newh* 1F **19**
Sun St. *W'vle* 6C **20**
Sussex Rd. *Burt T* 2J **17**
Sutton La. *Etw* 1C **6**
Sutton La. *Hatt* 3D **4**
Sutton La. *Hilt* 1H **5**
Swadlincote La. *Cas G* 7E **18**
Swadlincote Rd. *W'vle* 5A **20**
Swainspark Ind. Est. *Over* 2J **23**
Swallow Dale. *Thri* 2E **28**

Swallow Rd. *W'vle* 5C **20**
Swan Ct. Burt T *4A* ***14***
(off Ashby Rd.)
Swan Ct. Burt T *5J* ***13***
(off Orchard St.)
Swannington Heritage Trail. **5B** 28
Swannington Rd. *Coal* 1A **34**
Swannington St. *Burt T* 1G **13**
Swannington Towermill. **2A** 28
Swannymote Rd. *Whit & Belt* 3H **29**
Swan Wlk. *Burt T* 5J **13**
Swan Way. *Coal* 2G **35**
Sweethill. *Moi* 4D **24**
Swepstone Rd. *Heat* 7D **32**
Swepstone Rd. *Mea* 5H **31**
Swift Clo. *W'vle* 5C **20**
Swifts Clo. *Ibs* 6B **34**
Swinfen Clo. *Elli* 6D **34**
Swithland Rd. *Coal* 2K **35**
Sycamore Av. *Newh* 1H **19**
Sycamore Clo. *Burt T* 3K **17**
Sycamore Clo. *Etw* 1D **6**
Sycamore Clo. *Ibs* 7A **34**
Sycamore Clo. *L'tn* 4E **22**
Sycamore Ct. *Will* 1J **11**
Sycamore Dri. *Ash Z* 2C **26**
Sycamore Dri. *Moi* 3E **24**
Sycamore Rd. *Burt T* 3K **17**
Sycamore Rd. *Coal* 2H **35**
Sydney St. *Burt T* 1J **13**

T

Tailby Dri. *Will* 1H **11**
Talbot La. *Swan & Whit* 2C **28**
Talbot Pl. *Doni* 2B **30**
Talbot St. *Chur G* 6H **19**
Talbot St. *Whit* 3E **28**
Tamworth Rd. *Ash Z* 5K **25**
Tamworth Rd. *Mea* 7B **30**
Tandy Av. *Moi* 4E **24**
Tanner's La. *Rep* 3J **11**
Tan Yd. *Swan* 4C **28**
Tara St. *Bar H* 6J **35**
Tarquin Clo. *Stret* 4K **9**
Tatenhill La. *Bran* 1C **16**
Tatenhill La. *Tat* 7A **12**
Tavistock Clo. *Hug* 4D **34**
Taylor Clo. *Moi* 5D **24**
Teal Clo. *Coal* 2G **35**
Tean Clo. *Burt T* 6B **14**
Telmah Clo. *Stret* 5J **9**
Templars Way. *Whit* 4G **29**
Temple Clo. *Burt T* 7J **9**
Temple Hill. *Whit* 3G **29**
Tennyson Av. *Swad* 2K **19**
Tennyson Clo. *Mea* 6E **30**
Tennyson Rd. *Burt T* 7J **9**
Tenth Av. *Burt T* 7D **12**
Tern Av. *W'vle* 5C **20**
Third Av. *Burt T* 6E **12**
Thirlmere. *Coal* 1K **35**
Thirlmere Gdns. *Ash Z* 5B **26**
Thomas Rd. *Whit* 4E **28**
Thornborough Rd. *Coal* 7D **28**
Thorndale. *Ibs* 7A **34**
Thornescroft Gdns. *Burt T* 1G **17**
Thornewill Dri. *Stret* 5A **10**
Thornham Gro. *Ibs* 6B **34**
Thornley St. *Burt T* 1H **13**
Thorn St. *W'vle* 6C **20**
Thorn St. M. *W'vle* 6C **20**
Thornton Clo. *Coal* 1K **35**
Thorntop Clo. *B'dby* 1E **24**
Thorntree Clo. *R'stn* 7A **28**
Thorn Tree La. *Bret* 7G **15**
(in two parts)
Thorn Tree La. *Newh* 1G **19**
Thorpe Clo. *Stape* 6D **14**
Thorpe Downs Rd. *Chur G* 7J **19**
Thrift Rd. *Bran* 7G **13**
Thrushton Clo. *Find* 4K **7**
Ticknall Rd. *Harts* 1E **20**
Tideswell Grn. *Newh* 3F **19**
Tinsell Brook. *Hilt* 4J **5**
Tintagel Clo. *Stret* 4K **9**
Tithe Clo. *Thri* 1D **28**
Tiverton Av. *Whit* 7H **29**
Top Mdw. *Mid* 1J **19**
Torrance Clo. *Bran* 2F **17**
Torrington Av. *Whit* 7H **29**
Totnes Clo. *Hug* 4D **34**
Totnes Clo. *Stret* 7J **9**
Toulmin Dri. *Swad* 4J **19**
Toulouse Pl. *Ash Z* 3K **25**
Tourist Info. Cen. **3A** 26
(Ashby-de-la-Zouch)
Tourist Info. Cen. **5J** 13
(Burton upon Trent)
Tourist Info. Cen. **1C** 34
(Coalville)
Tournament Way. *Ash Z* 1K **25**
Tower Gdns. *Ash Z* 3K **25**
Tower Rd. *Burt T* 5C **14**
Tower Rd. *Harts* 2D **20**
Townsend La. *Don H* 5C **34**
Trent Av. *Will* 1J **11**
Trent Bri. *Burt T* 4K **13**
Trent Bri. *Coal* 3H **35**
Trent Clo. *Will* 1K **11**
Trent Ind. Est. *Burt T* 3K **13**
Trent La. *Newt S* 6F **11**
Trent St. *Burt T* 6H **13**
Trent Ter. Burt T *4K* ***13***
(off Bridge St.)
Tressall Rd. *Whit* 6H **29**
Trevelyan Clo. *Burt T* 5D **14**
Trinity Clo. *Ash Z* 3K **25**
Trinity Ct. *Ash Z* 3A **26**
Trinity Gro. *Swad* 5J **19**
Tristram Gro. *Stret* 4K **9**
Troon Clo. *Stret* 5H **9**
Truro Clo. *Mid* 3B **20**
Trusley Clo. *Bran* 1G **17**
Tudor Clo. *Ash Z* 4A **26**
Tudor Hollow. *Stret* 6J **9**
Tudorhouse Clo. *Newh* 1H **19**
Tudor Way. *Newh* 2H **19**
Turnbury Clo. *Bran* 1F **17**
Turolough Rd. *Whit* 2F **29**
Tutbury Castle. **6A** 4
(Remains of)
Tutbury Clo. *Ash Z* 4B **26**
Tutbury Crystal. ***7B*** *4*
(off Burton St.)
Tutbury Mus. **7B** 4
Tutbury Rd. *Rol D & Burt T* 4E **8**
Twayblade. *Bran* 7G **13**
Tweentown. *Don H* 5D **34**
Twentylands. *Rol D* 2J **9**
Twyford Clo. *Coal* 1K **35**
Twyford Clo. *Swad* 6G **19**
Twyford Clo. *Will* 1K **11**
Twyford Rd. *Will* 7J **7**
Tynefield Ct. *Etw* 3C **6**
Tynefield M. *Etw* 3C **6**
Tythe, The. *Mid* 1J **19**

U

Uldale Gro. *Chur G* 7K **19**
Ulleswater Cres. *Ash Z* 5B **26**
Underhill Wlk. *Burt T* 5J **13**
Union Pas. *Ash Z* 3A **26**
Union Rd. *Swad* 3J **19**
Union St. *Burt T* 5J **13**
Unity Clo. *Chur G* 7H **19**
Uplands Rd. *Mea* 6F **31**
Up. Church St. *Ash Z* 3B **26**
Up. Packington Rd. *Ash Z* 5B **26**
Uppingham Dri. *Ash Z* 2K **25**
Utah Clo. *Hilt* 3K **5**
Uttoxeter Rd. *Fos & Hatt* 2A **4**
Uxbridge Pleasure Ground. **6G** 13
Uxbridge St. *Burt T* 6H **13**

V

Vale Rd. *Harts* 5D **20**
Vale Rd. *Mid* 2J **19**
Valley Ri. *Swad* 3H **19**
Valley Rd. *Ibs* 7A **34**
Valley Rd. *Over* 6H **23**
Valley Way. *Whit* 4E **28**
Vancouver Dri. *Burt T* 4D **14**
Vaughan St. *Coal* 2D **34**
Verdon Cres. *Coal* 1J **35**
Vere Clo. *Will* 1J **11**
Vernon Ter. *Burt T* 3H **13**
Vicarage Clo. *B'dby* 7F **21**
Vicarage Clo. *Burt T* 3C **14**
Vicarage Fld. Burt T *6A* ***14***
(off Stapenhill Rd.)
Vicarage Gdns. *Swad* 4K **19**
Vicarage La. *Pack* 7A **26**
Vicarage Rd. *Swad* 4K **19**
Vicarage Rd. *W'vle* 6B **20**
Vicarage St. *Whit* 4G **29**
Victoria Clo. *Whit* 4E **28**
Victoria Cres. *Burt T* 2H **13**
Victoria Rd. *Burt T* 3H **13**
Victoria Rd. *Coal* 1E **34**
Victoria Rd. *Ibs* 5B **34**
Victoria St. *Burt T* 3H **13**
Victoria Vs. *Newh* 2H **19**
Viking Bus. Cen. *W'vle* 5C **20**
Violet La. *Burt T* 7A **14**
Violet Way. *Burt T* 7A **14**
Vulcan Ct. *Coal* 7E **28**
Vulcan Way. *Coal* 7E **28**

W

Waggon La. *Bret* 6G **15**
Wainwright Rd. *Hug* 4E **34**
Wakefield Av. *Tut* 7A **4**
Wakefield Dri. *Whit* 4F **29**
Wakelyn Clo. *Hilt* 3H **5**
Walford Rd. *Rol D* 2J **9**
Walker Rd. *Bar H* 6K **35**
Walker St. *Burt T* 6G **13**
Wall Rd. *Bran* 7F **13**
Walnut Clo. *Newh* 3H **19**
Walton Clo. *Swad* 6H **19**
Walton Rd. *Drake* 3H **17**
Warren Clo. *Stret* 5K **9**
Warren Dri. *L'tn* 3C **22**
Warren Hills Rd. *Coal* 6K **29**
Warren La. *Bran* 1E **16**
Warren La. *Whit* 2G **29**
Warwick Clo. *Bran* 7E **12**
Warwick Clo. *Mid* 2B **20**
Warwick St. *Burt T* 1H **13**
Warwick Way. *Ash Z* 4B **26**
Washford Rd. *Hilt* 4K **5**
Wash La. *R'stn* 2A **34**
Waterloo Pl. *Swad* 5J **19**
Waterloo St. *Burt T* 3H **13**
Waterside. *Burt T* 7K **13**
Waterside Rd. *Burt T* 2H **17**
Waterworks Rd. *Coal* 3H **35**
Watery La. *Bret* 4J **15**
Watery La. *Newh* 3E **18**
Watson St. *Burt T* 6J **13**
Wavenham Ct. *Hilt* 3H **5**
Waverley La. *Burt T* 4G **13**
Weathern Fld. *L'tn* 4E **22**
Wedgewood Clo. *Burt T* 6C **14**
Weir Bank. *Burt T* 2K **17**
Welford Ri. *Burt T* 7F **9**
Welland Clo. *Burt T* 2B **14**
Welland Clo. *Coal* 1J **35**
(Charnborough Rd.)
Welland Clo. *Coal* 2H **35**
(Nene Way)
Welland Rd. *Hilt* 4J **5**
Wellington Pk. *Burt T* 6F **13**
Wellington Rd. *Burt T* 6E **12**
Wellington St. *Burt T* 4G **13**
Wellington St. E. *Burt T* 4G **13**
Wellington St. W. *Burt T* 4G **13**
Well La. *B'dby* 7E **20**
Well La. *Rep* 5K **11**
Wells Rd. *Ash Z* 5J **25**
Wellwood Rd. *Newh* 2H **19**
Wentworth Dri. *Stret* 5J **9**
Wentworth Rd. *Coal* 2D **34**

Wesley Hillman Ct. Mea *5F* ***31***
(off Pegg's Clo.)
Westacre Dri. *Chur G* 6G **19**
West Av. *Hilt* 3H **5**
Western Av. *Coal* 7B **28**
Western Clo. *Ash Z* 5A **26**
Western Pk. *Ash Z* 5K **25**
Westfield Rd. *Burt T* 7G **9**
Westfield Rd. *Swad* 3J **19**
Westfields Av. *Ash Z* 3J **25**
Westfields Ter. *Ash Z* 2J **25**
West La. *Elli* 7J **35**
West Lawn. *Find* 3K **7**
Westminster Dri. *Stret* 6J **9**
Westminster Ind. Est. *Mea* 6E **30**
Westminster Way. *Ash Z* 1K **25**
Weston Pk. Av. *Burt T* 7K **9**
Weston St. *Swad* 5J **19**
West St. *Burt T* 4C **14**
West St. *Swad* 4J **19**
(in two parts)
West Wlk. *Ibs* 7B **34**
Westwood Pk. *Newh* 3G **19**
Wetherby Ct. *Bran* 1E **16**
Wetherel Rd. *Burt T* 5D **14**
Wetmore La. *Burt T* 1A **14**
Wetmore Rd. *Burt T* 1K **13**
(in two parts)
Wharf Rd. *Burt T* 2K **13**
Wharf Rd. Ind. Est. *Burt T* 2K **13**
Wheat Breach Clo. *Burt T* 1G **13**
Wheatlands. *Mid* 1J **19**
Wheatlands Rd. *Burt T* 1K **17**
Wheatley La. *Burt T* 3C **14**
Whetstone Dri. *Coal* 1F **35**
Whinchat Ct. Mea *6E* ***30***
(off Widgeon Dri.)
Whitehill Rd. *Elli* 7E **34**
Whitehouse Way. *Mea* 4F **31**
White Leys Ct. Coal *1D* ***34***
(off Melbourne St.)
Whitestone La. *A'lw* 5B **8**
Whitwick Bus. Pk. *Coal* 7F **29**
Whitwick Moor. *Thri* 2E **28**
Whitwick Rd. *Coal* 1E **34**
Wickets, The. *Burt T* 7A **14**
Wideshaft. *Swad* 4K **19**
Wigeon Dri. *Mea* 6E **30**
Wilfred Gdns. *Ash Z* 4K **25**
Wilfred Pl. *Ash Z* 4K **25**
Wilkes Av. *Mea* 6F **31**
Willars Way. *R'stn* 2A **34**
Willcock Rd. *Bran* 1F **17**
Willesley Clo. *Ash Z* 5J **25**
Willesley Gdns. *Ash Z* 5J **25**
Willesley Pk. Golf Course. **6J** 25
Willesley Rd. *W'sley & Ash Z* 7G **25**
Willesley Woodside. *W'sley* 4E **24**
(in two parts)
William Nadins Way. *Swad* 5F **19**
William Newton Clo. *Egg* 1C **10**
William St. *Burt T* 2H **13**
Willington La. *Egg* 6H **7**
Willington Rd. *Etw* 1C **6**
Willington Rd. *Find* 6K **7**
Willington Rd. *Rep* 2J **11**
Willington Rd. *Will* 7K **7**
Willn Clo. *Coal* 2J **35**
Willoughby Ho. *Swad* 4K **19**
Willowbrook Clo. *Ash Z* 1A **26**
Willow Brook Clo. *Hilt* 3H **5**
Willow Clo. *Mea* 4F **31**
Willow Clo. *Moi* 3E **24**
Willow Ct. *Swad* 4K **19**
Willow Dri. *Newh* 1G **19**
Willowfields. *Hilt* 3J **5**
Willow Grn. *Coal* 7K **29**
Willow Gro. *Will* 7H **7**
Willowpit La. *Hilt* 1K **5**
Willow Pl. *Burt T* 1K **17**
Willowsend Clo. *Find* 4K **7**
Willows, The. Burt T *5J* ***13***
(off Orchard Pk.)
Willow Way. *Ibs* 7A **34**
Wilmot Rd. *Swad* 5J **19**
Winchcombe Dri. *Burt T* 6C **14**
Winchester Ct. *Ibs* 6B **34**
Winchester Dri. *Burt T* 7H **13**
Winchester Dri. *L'tn* 4E **22**
Winchester Dri. *Mid* 2A **20**
Winchester Way. *Ash Z* 2K **25**
Windermere Av. *Ash Z* 4B **26**
Windmill Clo. *Ash Z* 4B **26**
Windmill Rd. *Etw* 2C **6**
Windmill St. *Chur G* 7H **19**
Windmill Vw. *Swan* 3B **28**
Windsor Clo. *Coal* 1J **35**
Windsor Clo. *Newh* 2H **19**
Windsor Dri. *Burt T* 6A **14**
Windsor Ind. Est. *Burt T* 2K **13**
Windsor Rd. *Ash Z* 4A **26**
Windsor Rd. *L'tn* 4E **22**
Winster Grn. *Newh* 3F **19**
Witham Clo. *Hilt* 3K **5**
Wolfscote Dale. *Chur G* 6G **19**
Wolsey Rd. *Coal* 7D **28**
Woodbine Clo. *Bran* 2D **16**
Woodcock Way. *Ash Z* 2B **26**
Wood Ct. *Burt T* 5J **13**
(James St.)
Wood Ct. *Burt T* 6H **13**
(Wood St., in two parts)
Wood Farm La. *W'vle* 4B **20**
Woodfield Dri. *Swad* 3K **19**
Woodhouse Rd. *Coal* 2J **35**
Woodhouse St. *W'vle* 5A **20**
Woodland Rd. *Stant* 2B **18**
Woodlands & Washlands Trail. **5B** 14
Woodlands Cres. *Over* 5H **23**
Woodlands Rd. *Over* 5J **23**
Woodlands Way. *Moi* 3E **24**
Wood La. *Newh* 1G **19**
Woodmans Cft. *Hatt* 4B **4**
(Appletree Rd.)
Woodmans Cft. *Hatt* 5B **4**
(Field Av.)
Woods Clo. *Hug* 4D **34**
Woodside. *Ash Z* 4J **25**
Woods La. *Burt T* 7A **14**
(in two parts)
Wood St. *Ash Z* 3B **26**
Wood St. *Burt T* 6H **13**
Wood St. *Chur G* 6J **19**
Woodview Rd. *Newh* 3E **18**
Woodville Rd. *Harts* 4C **20**
Woodville Rd. *Over* 6J **23**
Woodwards Pl. *Swad* 5K **19**
Woodward Way. *Swad* 4A **20**
Woolrooms, The. *Cole* 1A **28**
Woosnam Clo. *Bran* 2F **17**
Worcester Rd. *Burt T* 2K **17**
Wordsworth Av. *Swad* 3K **19**
Wordsworth Clo. *Burt T* 1J **13**
Wordsworth Clo. *Cole* 2K **27**
Wordsworth Way. *Mea* 7E **30**
Worthington Way. *Burt T* 5J **13**
Wortley Clo. *Coal* 1F **35**
Woulds Ct. Moi *3E* ***24***
(off Ashfield Dri.)
Wrekin Clo. *Ash Z* 5B **26**
Wren Clo. *W'vle* 5C **20**
Wren Pk. Clo. *Find* 4K **7**
Wyatt Rd. *Coal* 7F **29**
Wye Dale. *Chur G* 6G **19**
Wyggeston Rd. *Coal* 2E **34**
Wyggeston St. *Burt T* 1G **13**
Wyndham Cres. *Burt T* 4D **14**
Wyston Brook. *Hilt* 4J **5**

Y

Yard Clo. *Swad* 4J **19**
Yates Clo. *Moi* 4D **24**
Yeoman Ind. Est. *Burt T* 2K **13**
Yewtree Cres. *Burt T* 1A **18**
Yew Tree Rd. *Hatt* 3C **4**
Yewtree Rd. *Newh* 1G **19**
York Clo. *Mea* 5F **31**
York Clo. *Mid* 2A **20**
York Rd. *Chur G* 6J **19**
York St. *Burt T* 3H **13**

Z

Zetland Clo. *Coal* 2D **34**
Zion Hill. *Cole* 1B **28**